FRIEND

new concepts in housing

Mario Botta Mathias Klotz
Benson & Forsyth Norman Fos
de Moura Eugeen Liebaut Bj
FOBA Venturi, Thinking Space
Gumuchdjian Will Bruder Shin
Architects John Pawson Akira
Tom Maine-Morphosis José Cr
V Ranieri eok: eichinger oder
Rune Koh Kitayama Studio
Couvert & Guillaume Terve
Architects Daniele Marques
Scheithauer Gross Satoshi O
Valentiny et Associès Koen va
Esther Flavià Sean Godsell G.
Shiotsuka Patkau Architects Ro
Architekten Torsten Neeland B
& Livio Vacchini Adolf H. Kelz
Frank Marco Savorelli Patric

Benson & Forsyth Jun Aoki
ter & Partners Eduardo Souto
rne Mastenbroek & MVRDV
Architects Shigeru Ban Philip
akamatsu & Associates SCDA
akamoto Vincent van Duysen
z Ovalle Hiroyuki Arima Kuth
knechtl Claesson, Koivisto &
rchea Tadao Ando Fabienne
r Niall McLaughlin Circus
& Bruno Zurkirchen Kister
ada Architects Hermann &
n Velsen Araceli Manzano &
amonic et J.-C. Masson Takao
bert Oshatz Morger & Degelo
earth & Deplazes Silvia Gmür
& Hubert Soran Augustin +
Hernandez Ushida Findlay

Edition 2006

New concepts in housing

Work concept: Carles Broto
Publisher: Arian Mostaedi

Graphic design & production: Pilar Chueca

Text: Contributed by the architects, edited
by Jacobo Krauel and Amber Ockrassa

© Carles Broto i Comerma
Jonqueres, 10, 1-5
08003 Barcelona, Spain
Tel.: +34 93 301 21 99 Fax: +34-93-301 00 21
E-mail: info@linksbooks.net

Printed in China

new concepts in housing

structure

To think, design, create and build with a view toward the "new" necessarily involves introducing the unprecedented; it means throwing out the rule book, ignoring what you have always understood to be the "right" or "wrong" way to do things. "New" means always striving for innovation. This was the spirit we were looking for when compiling this ample collection of some of the best designs in house architecture the world over. We were looking for new interpretations, fresh viewpoints, innovations.

In short, we were looking for designs that were destined to determine the future of architecture. We are pleased with what we found.

Once the selection process was complete we decided that the presentation of the work had to include every angle of the architectural process, not just the photographs of the finished product. So, since technical know-how is just as important as artistic vision in any project, we have endeavored to touch upon every aspect in the design and construction process.

From conception to completion, you will find documentation on the materials used and construction processes - necessary complements to the design ideas of the contributing architects. Finally, since nobody is in a better position to comment on these projects than the creators themselves, we have included the architects' own comments and anecdotes.

So we are confident that we are leaving you in good, expert hands and that this selection of some of the finest, most innovative architectural solutions in the world will serve as an endless source of inspiration.

Hiroyuki Arima
House in Dazaifu

Dazaifu, Japan

This house is a device to provide natural views, and to include light into scenes of life positively. Here the value of space focuses on how to give man nature rather than functionality and efficiency as a place to live a life. That is, it is composed by the combination of some spaces resulting from the consideration of views, light and wind, and life thus follows the order of spaces determined in relation to the exterior. This residence therefore has a standard of value which is apparently different from the ordinary Japanese residence of today, and is much closer to the classical one.

The residence is located not too far from the approach to Dazaifu Shrine. The surroundings are silent and do not give the impression that one is close to a tourist spot. The ground here is uneven, and native bamboo groves and broadleaf trees provide pleasing views with the changing seasons. Two boxes are placed on the slope at a difference in level of 10 meters, facing the hills of Dazaifu. Each one is completely independent at its elevation.

The role of the lower box is to cut off the distant views horizontally and to expose the various changes of nature to the interior. Here, the views play an essential part in composing spaces as an element. The interior spaces have no concept of a room. The "box" forms a large room by itself. In it, the small boxes with functional elements, which form the unit arranging the function of life efficiently, are placed with order. The upper volume also reveals functional elements of the interior.

The upper box opens only vertically, and its role is to separate the interior from the exterior. It consists of two spaces, a light garden with a shallow pool of water, and beyond that Gallery 2. In this space, the resident can select various light shows by changing operable partitions. If necessary, the interior can be completely separated from the exterior. The visual relationship between man and nature in the upper volume is thus purer than in the lower volume.

The two boxes are connected by a natural path along the inclination of the slope. To live by coming and going between the two volumes means that a part of nature is naturally inserted into the living space.

Photographs: Koji Okamoto

Site plan

A vertical incision in the main volume of the dwelling provides natural lighting.

The dwelling consists of a single space inside which small containers house the most functional elements.

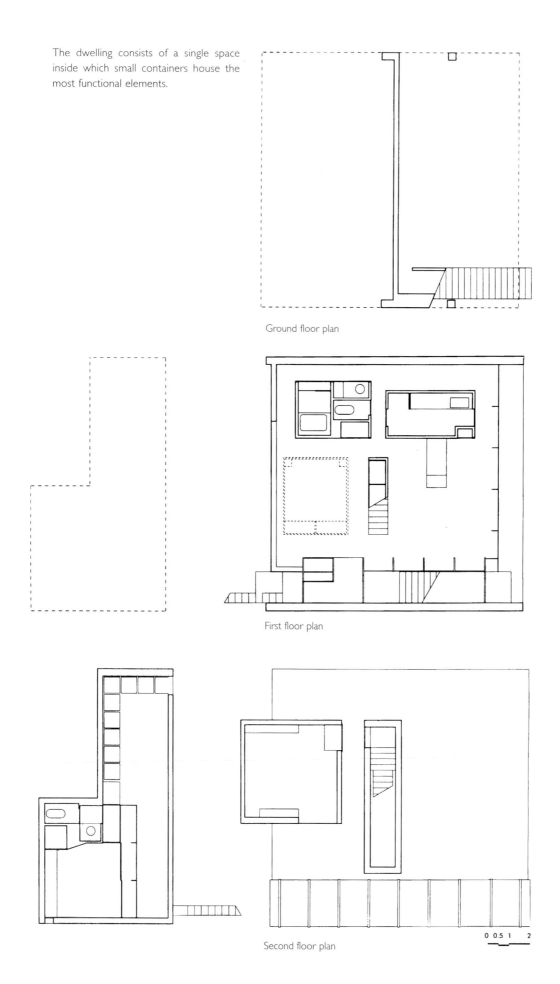

Ground floor plan

First floor plan

Second floor plan

0 0.5 1 2

14

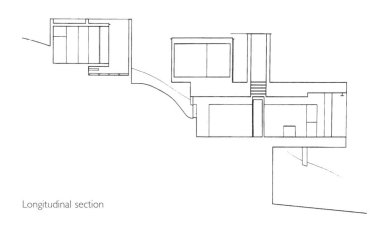

Longitudinal section

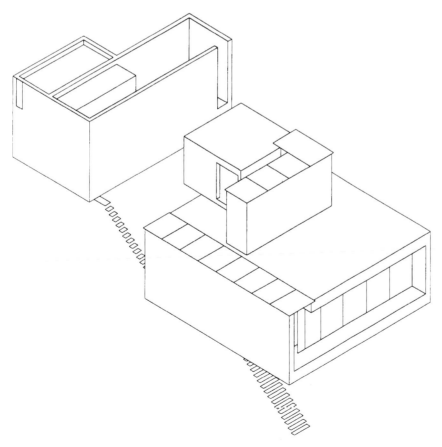

SCDA Architects
Teng Residence

Singapore, Singapore

This house, designed for a single male professional and his mother, is located on a tight suburban lot where plot ratios have been intensified and the height increased to three floors. One atypical feature of this home is the inclusion of a prayer/meditation room.

The suburbs of Singapore have been highly urbanized as the result of changes in zoning regulations. In the case of this project, the neighboring house is less than four meters away, making privacy a key concern.

The house is conceived as a latticed, two-story wooden box, constructed entirely of steel and wood and suspended above ground level.

A sheer wall (meant to form a visual barrier) has been built one meter from the building on the side facing a neighboring house. This one-meter slot allows light to wash against the sheer wall, reflecting it back toward the house.

All the plumbing and services are organized in a zone to the right of the party wall. A granite internal reflecting pool is located under the central, trellised skylight; while a slender steel and timber bridge connects the two halves of the program.

The facades are designed with a double skin. Fixed timber louvers are angled down to allow views of the exterior, while ensuring privacy from street level. The facade's glazing has openable panels allowing for natural ventilation.

Photographs: Peter Mealin

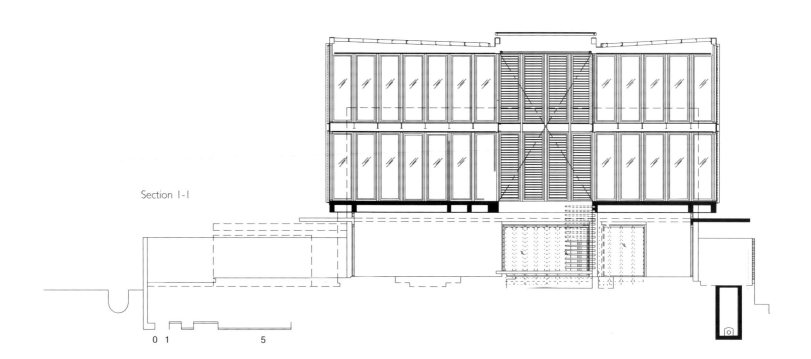

Section 1-1

0 1   5

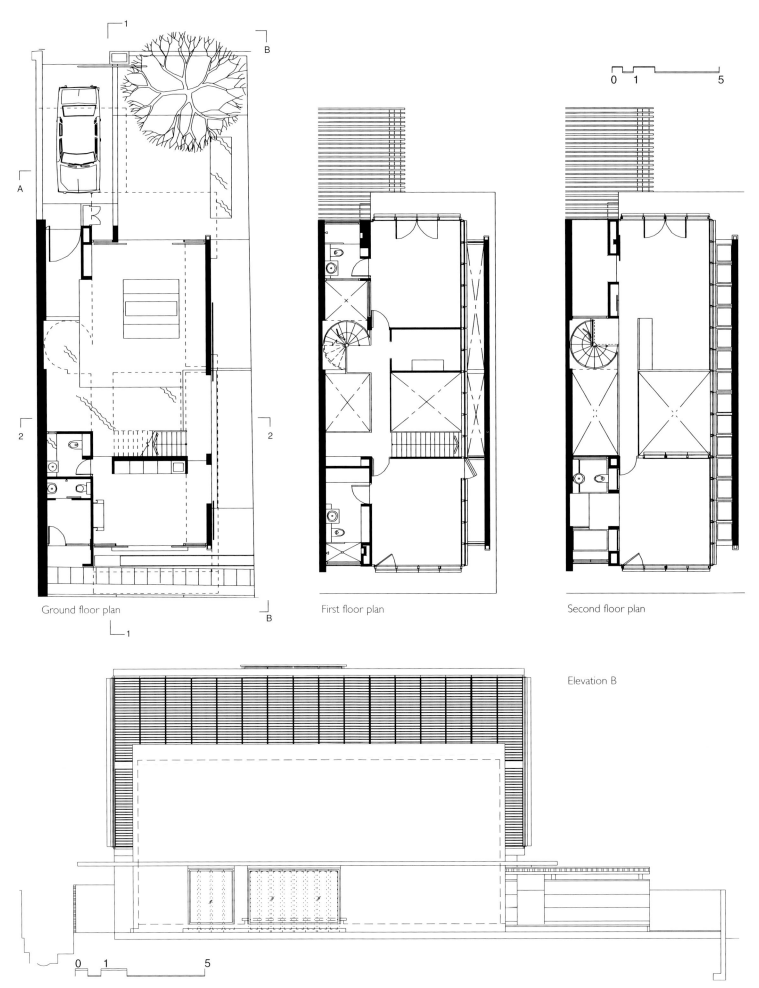

Ground floor plan

First floor plan

Second floor plan

Elevation B

0 1 5

0 1 5

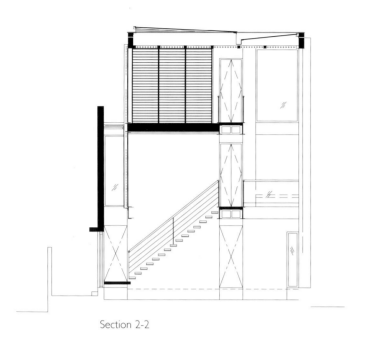

Section 2-2

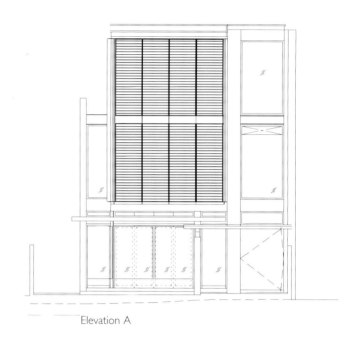

Elevation A

Only at ground level are the windows visually unobstructed to allow views of the narrow garden between the two houses. The living room is well-supplied with natural light from above (the central well) and the side. Light is increased by white walls and floor.

Floor-to-ceiling windows have been fitted with fixed, external wooden louvers to ensure privacy. A full garden was not possible on such a small lot, so greenery has been included wherever possible: the studio on the upper floor looks into a small patio.

Niall McLaughlin
Northamptonshire Shack

Northamptonshire, UK

This dwelling is located on agricultural land that was used as a reconnaissance base by the allied forces during the Second World War. The building was constructed manually, without any working drawings and in conjunction with a landscape scheme, so in its development the modifications were open to all those involved.

The client, a photographer specialized in insects and nature with back lighting and special effects, wanted a house that also served as a setting for his work. He therefore decided to regenerate an abandoned pond that was lost between a labyrinth of brambles and bushes. After the water had been filtered and oxygenated with plants, the brambles and bushes had been cleared away and the water had been populated with fish, the pond recovered its life and could attract the dragonflies and other animals that would be used as models for the photographer.

The form and the materials of the building were conceived with the intention of capturing and storing several types of light. Some external spaces, such as the south area facing the pond, are used as rooms in which objects could be placed for photographing under the required conditions. A long arm was also built over the pond to photograph insects on the surface with the water as a background. To take advantage of the geographical situation of this dwelling, the architect incorporated a sauna, a bedroom and a belvedere with views over the aquatic landscape and the surrounding grasslands.

The building combines wood, masonry, metal cladding and other elements, and a glass-fiber wing whose extended staircases of polycarbonate and perforated metal emerge from the water. Due to the curious external appearance, the access to the dwelling is like the entrance to a hidden cave.

The main elements of the structure are the numerous "wing" elements that crawl over the rear part of the building, the skylight that runs along the longitudinal axis, and a complex overhanging roof supported by fine metal angles laid out in a fan-shape that bend with the force of the strong wind that blows in this area.

Photographs: Nicholas Kane

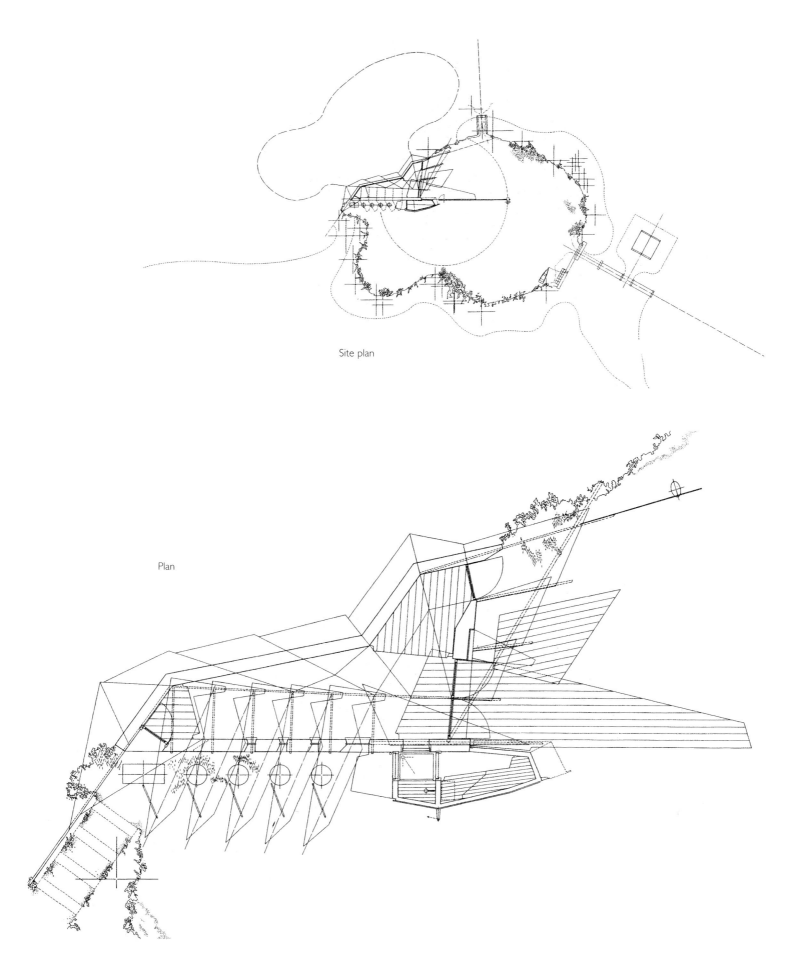

Site plan

Plan

The effects of light on the exterior are supplemented inside the dwelling by means of the incorporation of polycarbonate deflectors on the roof, just above the skylight. These are secured by fine rods and deviate the rays of light creating a pleasant illumination.

Circus Architects
Vaight Apartment

London, UK

The loft has been formed by knocking together two shell spaces to provide one substantial double-height volume, of a scale rarely to be found in central London, where it is located. Carved from the muscular confines of an old printing house the space comes with thick concrete columns and down stand beams and galvanized steel windows of industrial size.

In order to accommodate a family of four, the brief asked for three bedrooms, three bathrooms and as much double space as possible.

The solution found by the architects involves the piling up of bedrooms towards the back of the space against the window walls wherever possible.

This spatial organization creates a bright and open space that allows an unconventional way of living. The kitchen area penetrates into the living and dining area, next to closed free-standing volume, which encloses a small study. The upper-level living area overlooks these spaces.

Photographs: Richard Glover

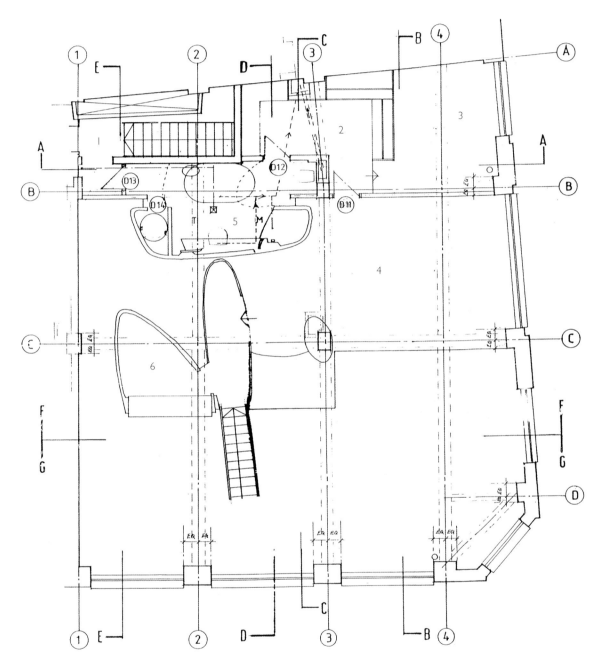

Upper floor plan

1. Existing fire escape
2. Dressing room
3. Master bedroom
4. Upper reception (on mezzanine)
5. Master bathroom
6. Study

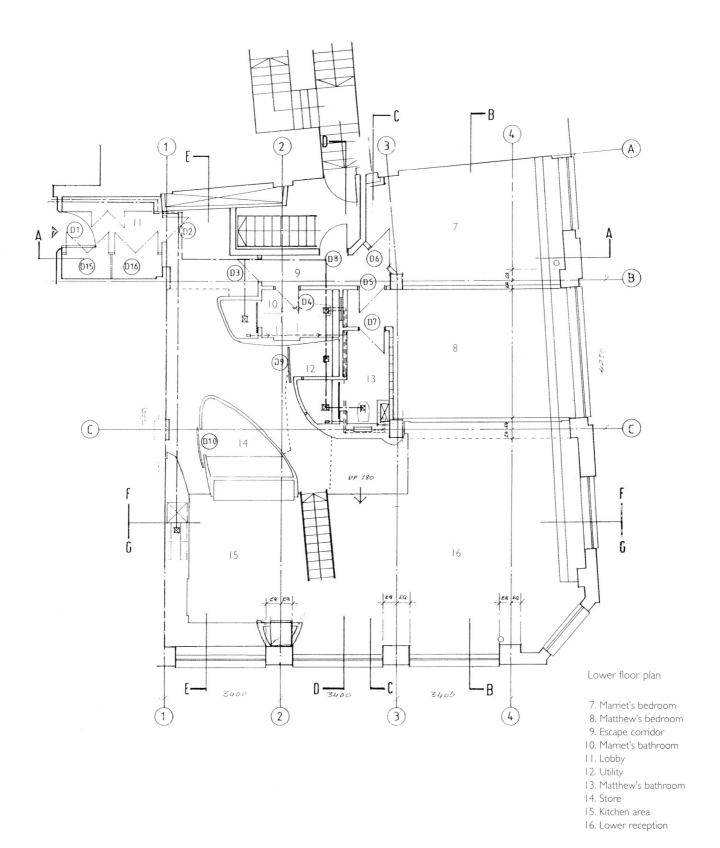

Lower floor plan

7. Marriet's bedroom
8. Matthew's bedroom
9. Escape corridor
10. Marriet's bathroom
11. Lobby
12. Utility
13. Matthew's bathroom
14. Store
15. Kitchen area
16. Lower reception

Section CC

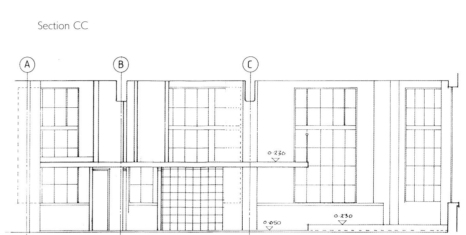

Section DD

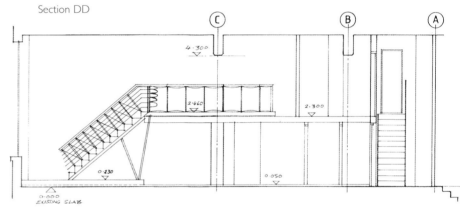

Section EE

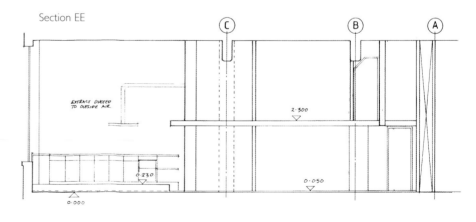

Sean Godsell
Carter / Tucker House

Breamlea, Australia

A three level, three bedroom, 12m X 6m box was embedded into the side of a sand dune. The lower ground floor is for guests and the single space can be divided by a sliding wall into two rooms if so required. Similarly the single space on the middle level can also be divided to separate the owner's bedroom from a small sitting area. The top floor is for living and eating and takes advantage of views across a rural landscape.

In traditional Chinese architecture the aisle is a fluid outer building which is continuous around the perimeter of the inner building. In traditional Japanese architecture the aisle (gejin) is not continuous when added to a structure, but is fluid space when an inner building is partitioned (hedate) to cause an aisle to be formed.

The traditional outback Australian homestead is also surrounded by fluid space (the verandah) which is sometimes partly enclosed with flywire or glass to form an indoor/outdoor space (sunroom). Where in cooler climates the roof of the aisle provides shelter from snow and rain, in the outback the verandah helps shade the vertical surfaces of the building from direct solar radiation. The Carter/Tucker house is primarily an investigation of the verandah/aisle and its potential as an iconic element common between eastern and western architecture.

The verandah exists in this house in an abstracted form. On all three levels the outer (timber screen) skin of the building tilts open and forms a verandah on the perimeter of the building. This component allows the fluidity of the aisle space to transfer itself across the façade of the building.

On the middle level, the bedroom then becomes the verandah while the corridor, formed by the insertion of a service core, becomes the inner room. Depending on the time of the year the verandah can then be enclosed with sliding flyscreens to become a sunroom, or left open.

The bedroom space can then be further modified by the operation of the hedate wall which when drawn across the bedroom forms an inner building within the aisle. The idea of fluid space is further emphasized by the service core being kept free from both ends of the building so that movement through the floor is continuous - no steps have to be retraced.

Photographs: Earl Carter

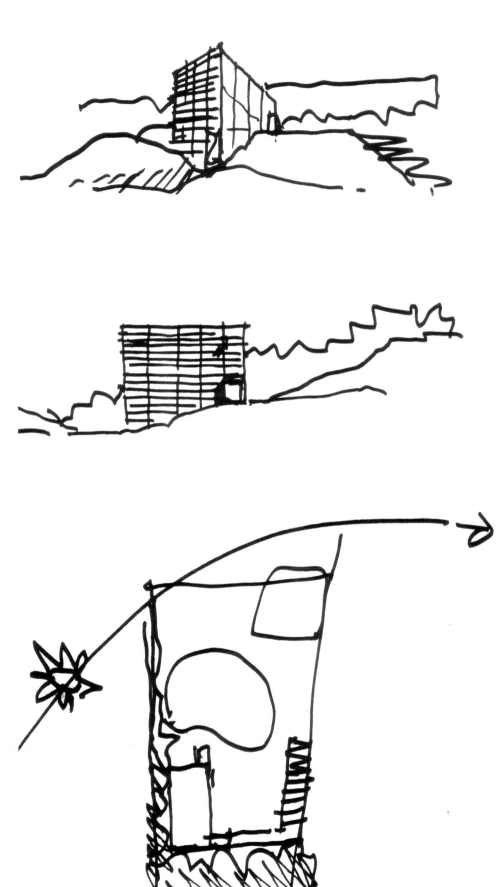

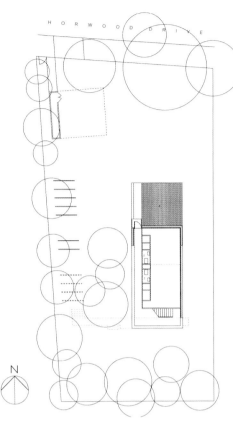

The façades are veiled with a system of adjustable louvers which blur the edges of the building and constantly modify its appearance depending upon the position of the viewer. Light enters or is prevented from entering the building in a constantly changing way.

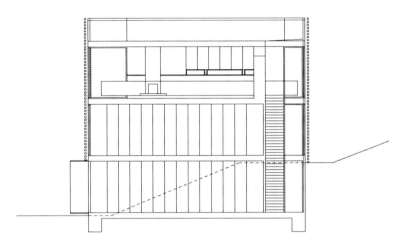

Site plan

Section

The verandah exists in this house in an abstracted form. Elements of the object exist throughout the building while its traditional form is not immediately evident. On all three levels the outer, timber-screen skin of the building tilts open to create a verandah on the perimeter of the building. The horizontal plane of the ceiling is thus extended beyond the building line.

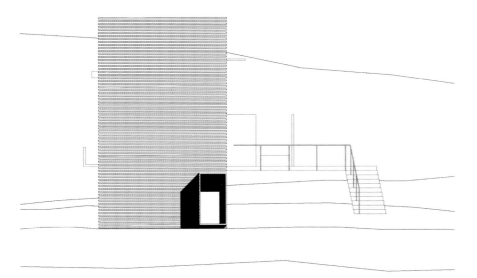

North elevation

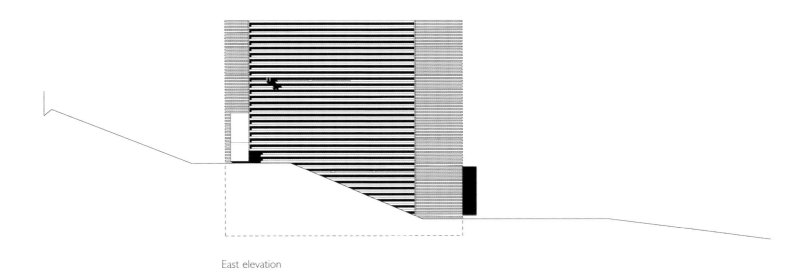

East elevation

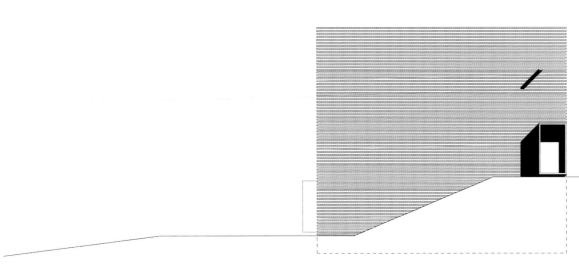

West elevation

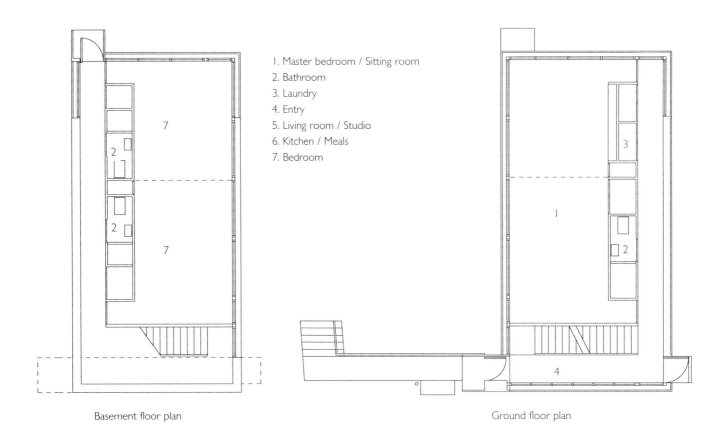

1. Master bedroom / Sitting room
2. Bathroom
3. Laundry
4. Entry
5. Living room / Studio
6. Kitchen / Meals
7. Bedroom

Basement floor plan

Ground floor plan

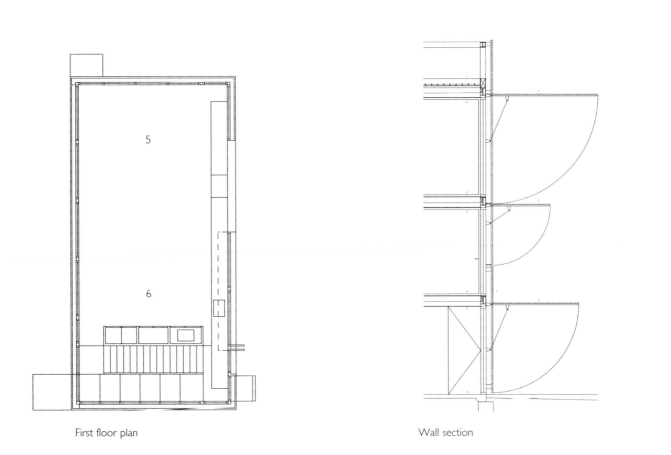

First floor plan

Wall section

Adolf H. Kelz & Hubert Soran
Mittermayer's House

Salzburg, Austria

In the conversion of this two-century-old house near Salzburg the architects have combined two approaches. The original building was divided into two main parts: the original stone building and a wooden shed. The stone building and its internal distribution have been conserved, but the shed has been converted into a big glass box with wooden joinery, within which the rooms hang from the hipped roof.

The glazed box which occupies approximately half of the main building forms the most radical aspect of this scheme. The structural elements of steel and wood are separated from the glazed skin. The living/dining area on the ground floor has an open plan and is overlooked by galleries, while the rooms are white plywood boxes, suspended in the space created within the glass box. All the spaces are independent units integrated into a whole and conjugated by spiral staircases, galleries and walkways that create exciting perspectives. The program includes four bedrooms for the owner's children, a library and a restroom.

The roof has been conserved almost intact, only interrupted by a strip window and a skylight for the loft. It tempers the contrast between old and new and brings unity to the whole. A small refurbished annex with a new zinc roof contains the garage, sauna and some utilities.

Photographs: Angelo Kaunat

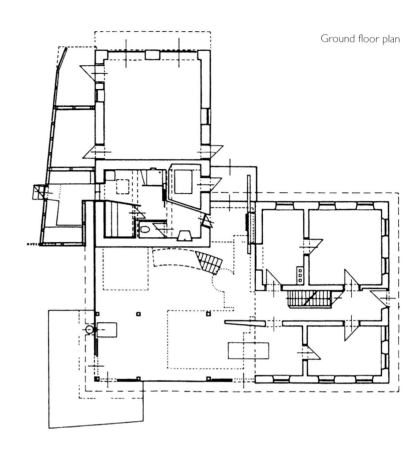

Ground floor plan

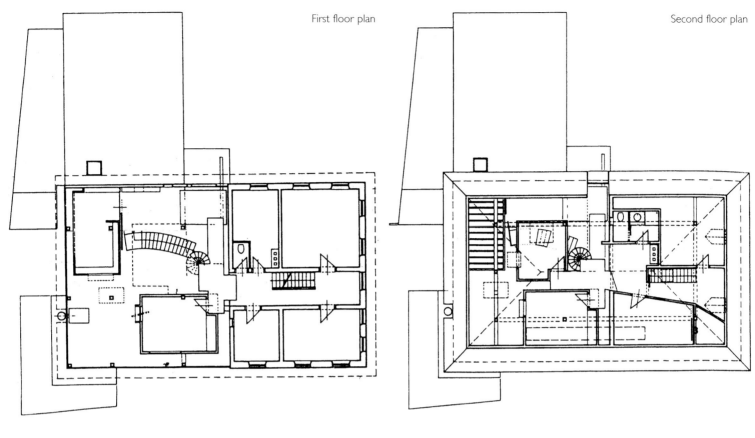

First floor plan   Second floor plan

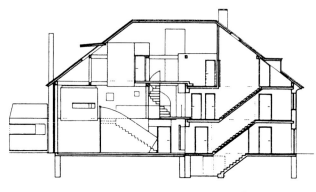

Cross section

The conventional circulation systems have been replaced by walkways, galleries and spiral staircases that connect the different spaces.

Views of the ground floor living area. The wood and steel structural elements do not touch the façade of the building.

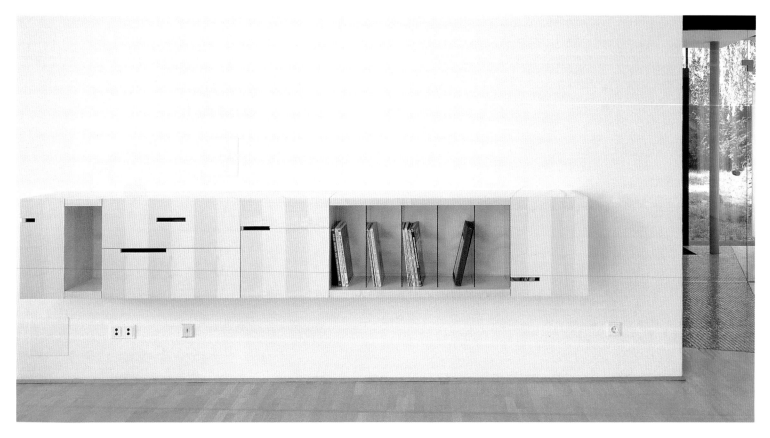

Silvia Gmür & Livio Vacchini
3 Single-Family Houses

Beinwil am See, Canton Argovia, Switzerland

Located in the Swiss town of Beinwil am see these three single-family modules stand out from the architecture of the area due to their special design and arrangement. Three identical dwellings located on a hillside with a view of the lake give form to a single complex. The different modules share their foundations in a kind of pedestal that determines part of their architectural character, enhancing their role in the landscape. The dwellings create a compositional rhythm in which the predominant geometry of the floors is the square, whereas in the elevations it is the rectangle. This rhythm is determined by a linear succession of "solids" and "voids" in which the former act as private spaces while the latter are used for the common living areas. The private space is divided in turn into porch and room, so the differentiation between exterior and interior is slightly blurred. The facades are composed of three differentiated elements that are used for their functionality and their aesthetic qualities: cement, glass and "air" that in the void is converted into matter. It is an architecture that tends towards the essential without expressive rhetoric or metaphoric language, an architecture without superfluous details in which the orientation becomes crucial through its form, structures and materials.

The generous use of natural light, a perfect organization of the spaces, the choice of specific materials, and the careful orientation of the structures are the basic ingredients of this work full of order and balance. These three dwellings not only produce multiplicity, variety, potentiality and virtuality, but also a way of inhabiting and combining private and common spaces.

Photographs: Vaclav Sedy

Ground floor plan

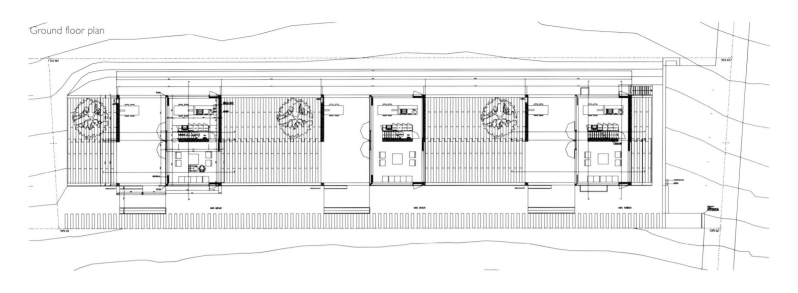

First floor plan

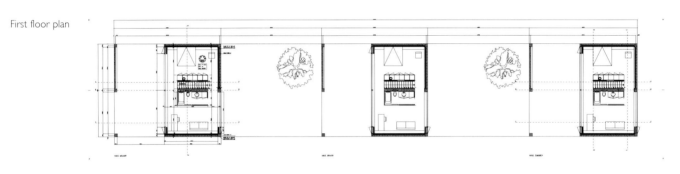

60

The elementary rhythm of the square-cube is added to the horizontal nature of the base on which the three dwellings are placed, creating an expressive and symphonic effect in which the different dimensions seem to mediate between the vertical and the horizontal, and between the solid and the void.

Standard elevation

Standard sections

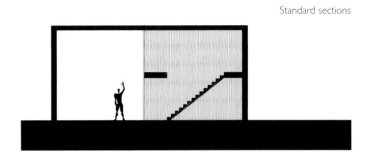

North-east elevation

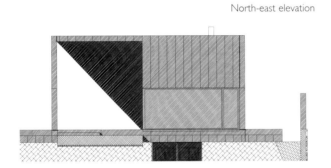

South-west elevation

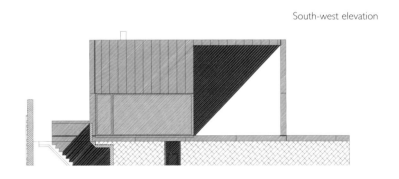

Standard floor plan

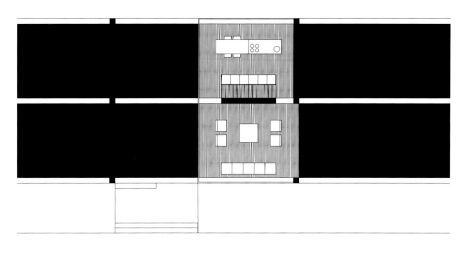

South-east elevation

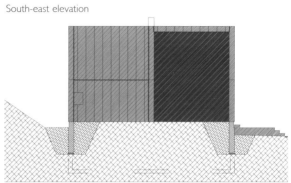

North-west elevation

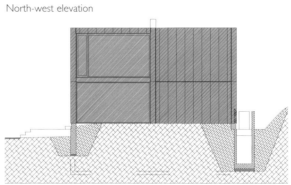

Vincent van Duysen
Town Houses in Flanders

Flanders, Belgium

The project consists of the refurbishment of a classic 1930's row house with a fairly restricted width and a deep plan.

The house is situated between five similar row houses by the same architect and from the same period; which is why the front elevation has only been restored instead of entirely redone.

The deep plan of the existing house made it very dark, so Van Duysen has instead opted for an open plan with a glazed central void over three stories, visually connecting all the spaces vertically and horizontally, with daylight pouring through a large rooflight and a completely glazed back elevation.

The impressive spatial qualities are emphasized by several factors. From one side, the unrestricted views from the front toward the back of the house on all levels (entering through the front door one can see the garden gate in the back garden). Views are also provided by two voids on the rooflight and the central lightwell; the completely glazed back elevation gives views of the old industrial buildings and chimneys.

The materials used in the building process consist of flush planes of dark tinted oak against a background of white plastered walls and have been carefully proportioned to emphasize the spatial system of the house. Large planes of glass divide the structure and organization of the plan.

The whole building is opened toward the garden through the completely glazed elevation, whereby the window frames again reflect the structure inside. At the same time, the walled garden elongates the space of the dining and cooking area and, combined with the void above the dining room and the use of identical stone flooring both outside and in, effectively pulls the internal and external space together into one unified whole. The patio wall marks the end of the external dining area and creates a kind of "garden room", with a framed view of the garden.

Photographs: Jan Verlinde

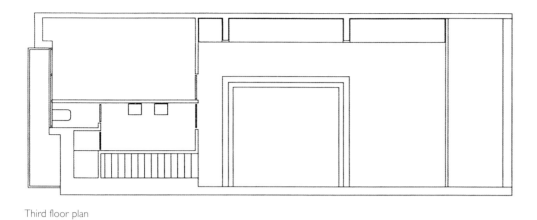

Third floor plan

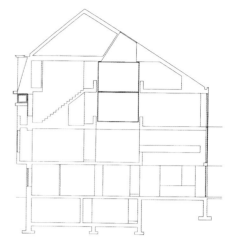

Cross section

Second floor plan

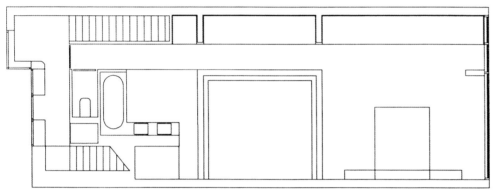

First floor plan

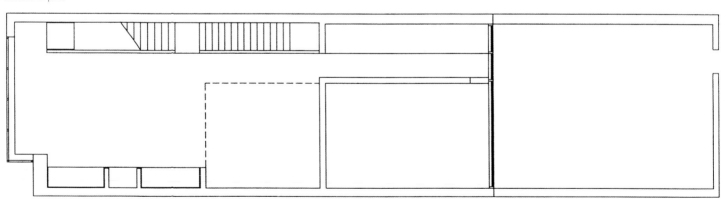

Ground floor plan

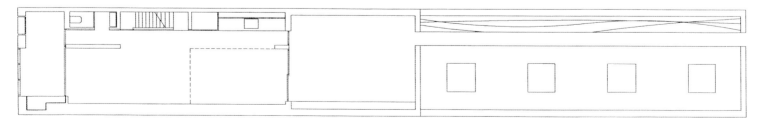

Eduardo Souto de Moura
Bom Jesus House

Braga, Portugal

Bom Jesus was shaped by a single design, in which two different levels are combined, each with different construction techniques. Indeed, the two houses were conceived and built as a single one.

The first level, for the children, consists of an *opus incertum*, a stone cube with doors and windows. The second level, that of the parents, is a concrete cube with a large glazed balcony.

The meticulous attention that Souto de Moura pays not only to architectural space and form, but also to the effects produced by the materials both in the interior and the exterior can be clearly appreciated in this project.

Photographs: Luis Ferreira Alves

75

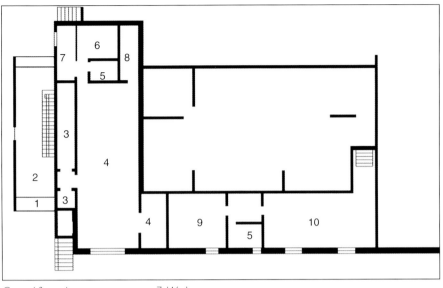

Ground floor plan
1. Access
2. Hall
3. Storage
4. Garage
5. WC
6. Staff

7. Wash room
8. Machine room
9. Bedroom
10. Living room
11. Dining room
12. Kitchen
13. Study

On the ground floor (the children's area) the use of traditional materials is predominant: stone, wood and clay tiles, which have been skilfully combined with a glass wall with aluminum profiles. The building details of this floor transmit the sensations of the different finishes: smooth, polished, rough, fragile, solid, natural, and artificial.

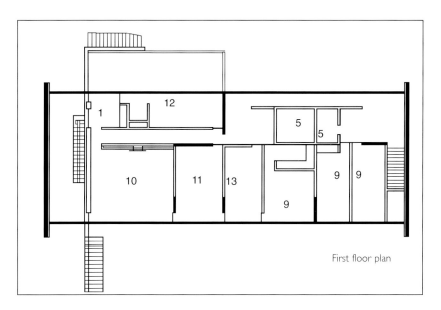

First floor plan

Koh Kitayama
Plane + House

Tokyo, Japan

This house, with an attached studio and a total floor area of 177m², occupies almost the entirety of its small plot, located in a densely populated area of Tokyo. The client is an industrial designer who required that the building include facilities for both a home and office.

Because of local zoning restrictions the construction area is an exact square, which at least offers the possibility of creating wide-open, diaphanous spaces. The building is an equal span rigid-frame structure with supporting columns on the inside, freeing up space in the hallways.

The space formed between the outer and inner walls is used for staircases, and also serves as a ventilation duct. Top-lit glass has been installed in the ceiling in this space, guiding natural light downwards.

This structure displays the planar format of homes often seen in Asia, with hallways running around the outside of the living areas. Such spaces are easily adaptable to changes in daily living.

However, in other aspects, the architects have consciously tried to distance the design of this biulding from typical Japanese architecture. They feel that in the past several years, particularly in Japan, there has been a trend towards an almost unnatural sterility and homogeneity, reminiscent of the brightly-lit convenience store equipped with air conditioning and heating. Homes in which spatial composition and environment-friendly technology support one another are not -but perhaps shoud be- the norm. As a response, they have designed a home in which the occupants must recognize when it is time for a "change of clothes", opening and closing household fixtures according to the given climate and season.

Photographs: Nobuaki Nakagawa

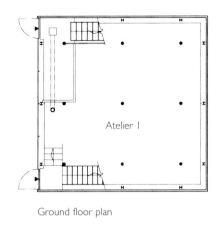

Ground floor plan

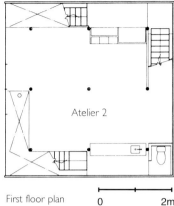

First floor plan

0   2m

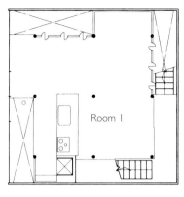

Second floor plan

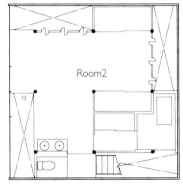

Third floor plan

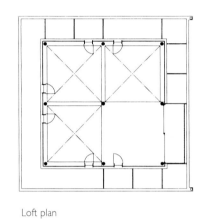

Loft plan

Due to zoning laws, the construction space is an exact square, a limitation which nonetheless gave rise to the creation of wide-open spaces. Hallways and stairways have been placed on the periphery of the living areas.

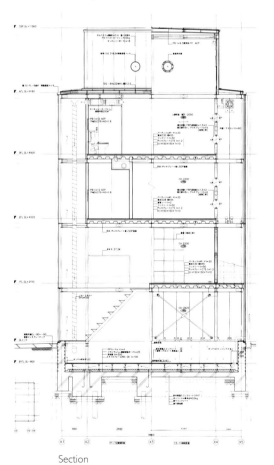

Section

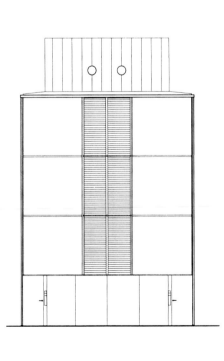

Elevation

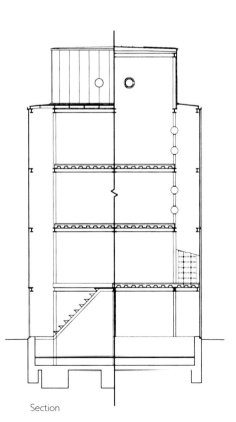

Section

Claesson, Koivisto & Rune
Apartment in Stockholm

Stockholm, Sweden

The task confronting this team of three architects was how to create a comfortable, uncluttered living space in a very small area. The apartment, located in the center of Stockholm, has a total floorspace of just 33.5 m² containing basically one open-plan room, with adjoining concrete-tiled terrace and blue mosaic-tiled bathroom, connected to the main room by a small opening with a sliding acid-etched window.

In spite of its size, the apartment has all the necessary conveniences. Non-living space (storage, dishwasher, refrigerator, freezer, microwave) is all either built-in or concealed behind doors, resulting in a serene and minimalist aesthetic in which to carry on domestic life. Although the work of several designers has been used in the finished project, all the built-in furnishings were designed by the architects themselves.

The terrace furniture can easily be lifted inside for occasions demanding more seating space, and the futon bed doubles up as a sofa. All the lighting and two motorized Venetian blinds are controlled from one centrally placed panel. The Venetian blinds, when shut, hide both the windows and the work desk.

Photographs: Patrick Engquist

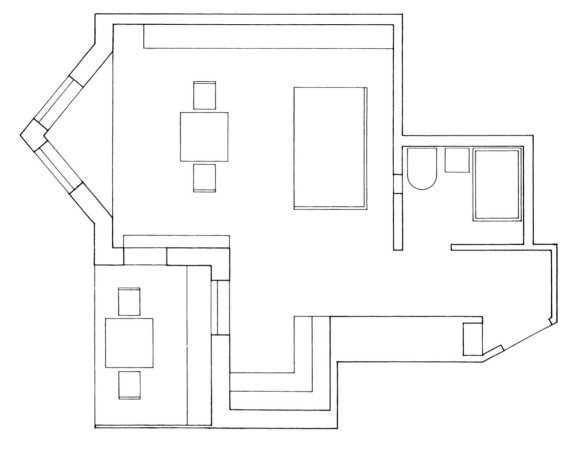

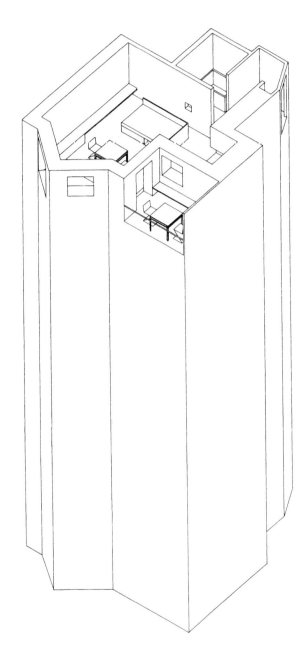

The dwelling is ordered around a small single room, but the architects have managed to give the apartment full visual and spatial opening.

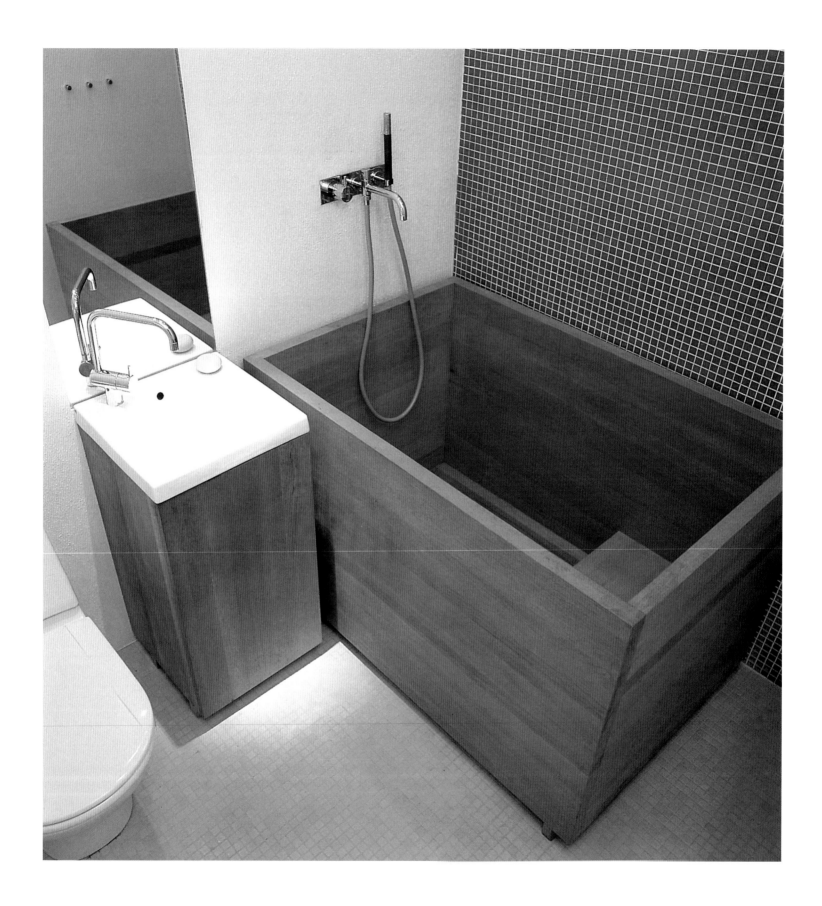

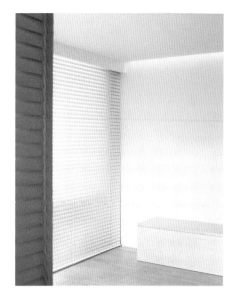

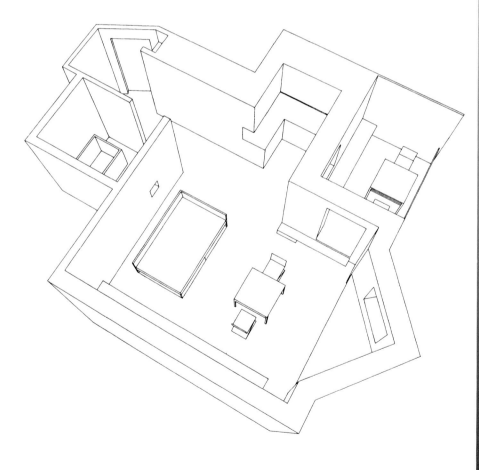

Thinking Space Architects
House on Club Row London

London, UK

This house had been a vacant site since the four-story building previously occupying the site (built in 1840) was demolished in 1957. It is surrounded on three boundaries by existing structures. To the north is a substantial three-story warehouse building with smaller, converted two- and three-story residential buildings to the east and south. These smaller buildings have windows facing the boundaries, and there is an existing right of way for a fire escape running across the site. These constraints, combined with limited space (62 sq m), meant that the property had been passed over by developers, and was deemed unusable for anything other than a parking lot.

The house aims to participate in the street and draw on its generosity. For this reason the house is highly glazed and open on the main street elevation. The Georgian houses on the adjacent street were an important precedent with their simple geometry and large openings. To overcome the lack of external views and height restrictions imposed by zoning laws, an atrium plan was developed. This creates quiet, secluded bedrooms (the street is on a bus route), stacked at the rear of the house on the ground and first floors, with a sequence of more public living spaces rising from the basement to the roof terrace. On the north side a service zone is generated by the stair well, which provides storage and areas for the kitchen and showers.

This simple design scheme creates clear volumes which are linked and dramatically lit by the atrium allowing all the rooms to participate in this south-facing home, with its sensation of spaciousness in a relatively limited space.

The basement acts as a raft foundation, removing the need for deep foundations with the stub spine walls at the front and, adjacent to the stairs, strengthening the existing party wall and providing cross bracing to the structure.

Photographs: Edmund Sumner

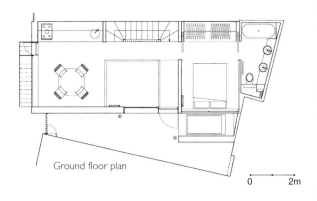

Ground floor plan

0   2m

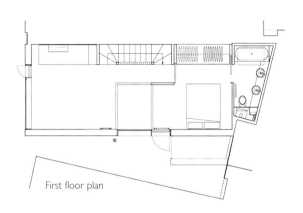

First floor plan

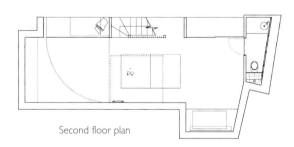

Second floor plan

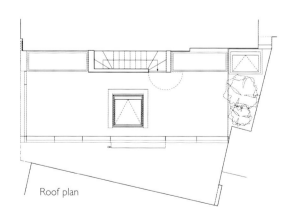

Roof plan

91

Elevation

0   2m

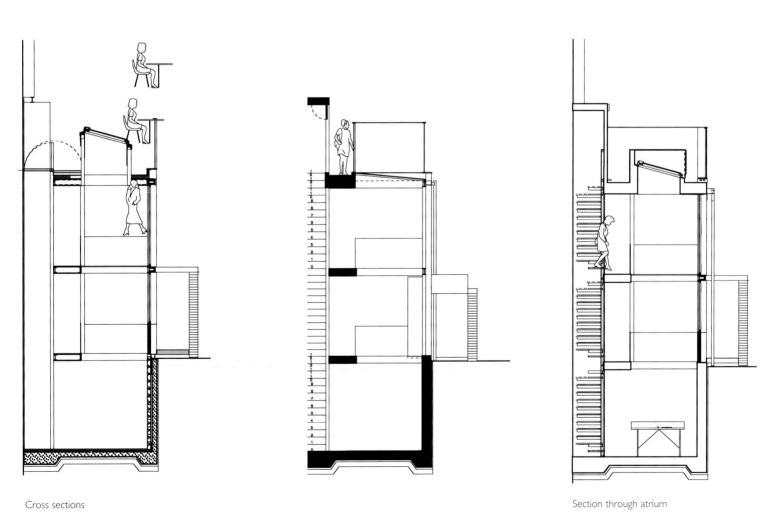

Cross sections

Section through atrium

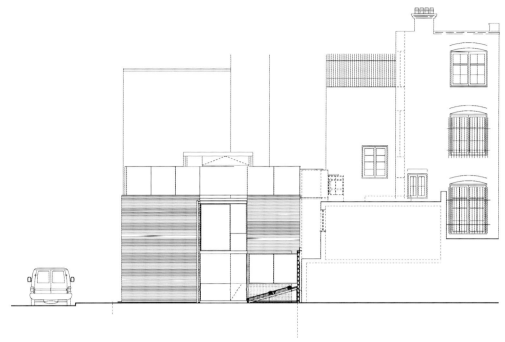

South elevation

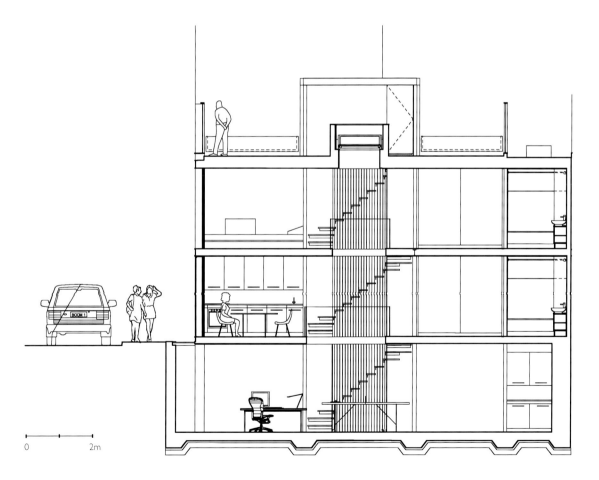

0   2m

Longitudinal section

93

Kister Scheithauer Gross
Mach House

Dessau-Mosigkau, Germany

The building is designed as a single-family home with an integrated fully separate apartment. It has a total residential floor area of approx. 170 m² (119 m²+52 m²) and is based on an ecological energy-use concept making it almost autonomous in terms of external power needs. A determining design factor was the location of the building. The site had been originally occupied by a market gardening operation. Starting out from an ecological low-energy concept that was to be reflected in the projected building's character, it was decided to make use of greenhouse building traditions. A rural building approach has been adopted, but interpreting it as a technically innovative residential building which exercises a pilot function in its present configuration. The facade presents itself to an approaching observer as a decorative concrete wall with a large wooden gate behind which an arrangement of interior yards, separate for the residential parties, divide the access wall and the actual building. As a result, the house retains a discreet presence when viewed from the road, remaining concealed behind trees and opening itself to the visitor via a sequence of paths that lead across an array of squares and yards.

The inner building core is formed by two load-bearing concrete walls with stiffening function, which are presented as decorative concrete surfaces. Comprised between them is the central corridor on the ground floor and the central technical room arranged on the upper level. The building has no basement.

The exterior building front consists of a structure of glue laminated timber uprights with Betoplan (epoxy-coated plywood) panel bracing. The panels are fixed, with reddish shadow joints for contrast, or provided in the form of movable wooden shutters in front of the windows.

The single-pitch roof slopes towards the west and consists entirely of double-web Macrolon panels with wooden hinged slats. The roof slat position is selected to ensure that the low winter sun will heat the air above the collector chamber to provide room heating via a heat exchange process.

Photographs: Martin Classen

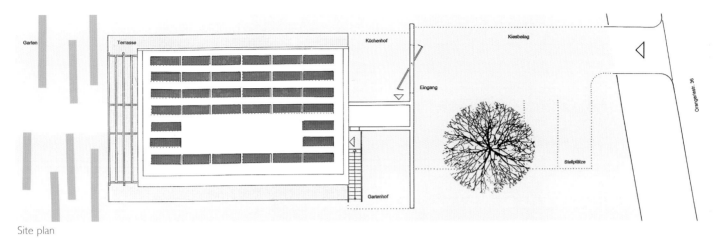

Site plan

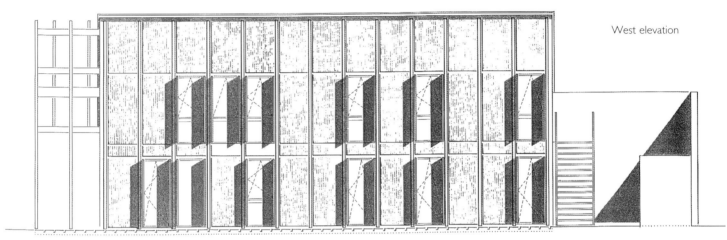

West elevation

The tradition in greenhouse building was the departure point for this project, which is based on an autonomous ecological concept and aims to handle the dwelling's energy needs on a self-sufficient basis, free from outside help.

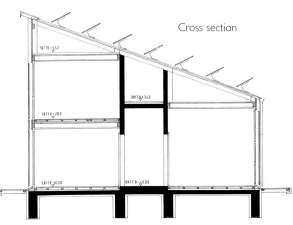

Cross section

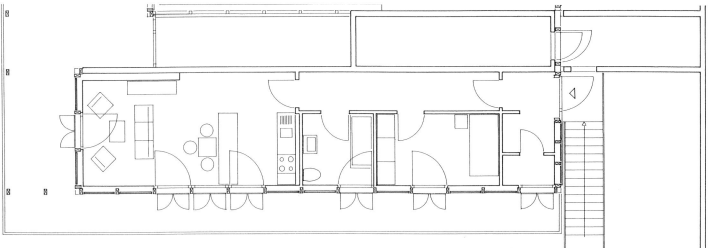

First floor plan

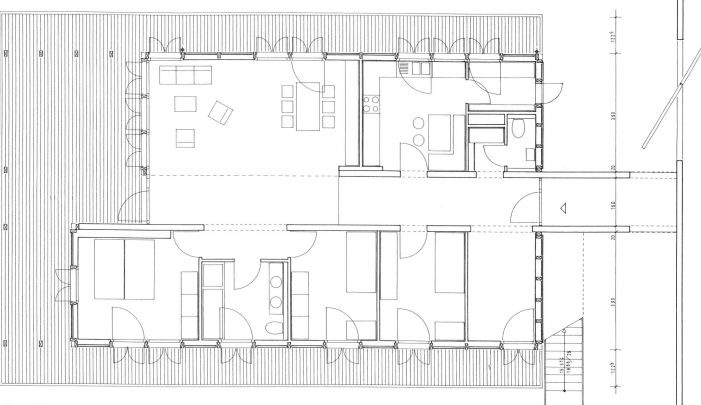

Ground floor plan

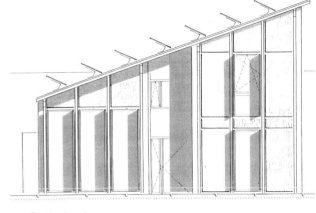

South elevation

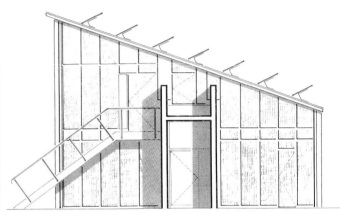

North elevation

Construction detail

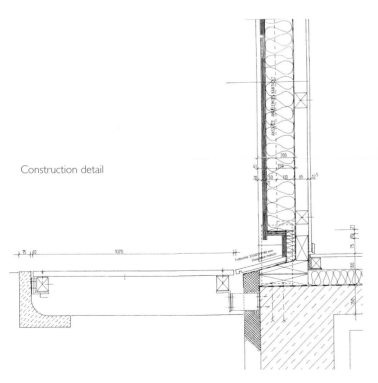

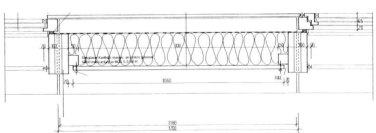

Horizontal section of the facade element (closed)

Detail of shutters

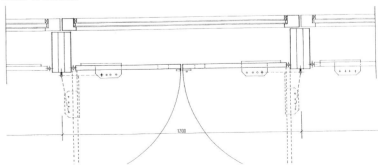

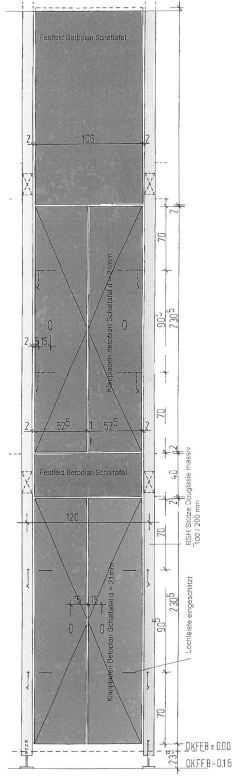

Festfeld Betoplan Schaltafel

2 | 106 | 2

70

Klappladen Betoplan Schaltafel d = 21 mm

90⁵ | 230⁵

2 5 15

2 | 52⁵ | 1 | 52⁵ | 2

70

Festfeld Betoplan Schaltafel

120

40

70

BSH Stütze Douglasie massiv
100 / 200 mm

90⁵ | 230⁵

15 15

Lochleiste eingeschlitzt

Klappladen Betoplan Schaltafel d = 21 mm

70

OKFFB ± 0.00
OKFFB -0.16
23⁵

Satoshi Okada Architects
Villa Man-Bow

Atami, Japan

This project is a villa located in the mountains of Atami, a famous spa resort on the Pacific Ocean, about 100 km west of Tokyo. The plot is on a steep and rocky mountain ridge, with a grade of approximately 70 degrees, facing north to splendid views of the ocean beyond the valley down below. It is some 9 meters above the front street, which, in general, makes for difficult building conditions. To make matters worse, the area is noted for strong winds, high humidity and dense fogs, as well as frequent earthquakes. In particular, the salty gales blowing up through the narrow valley from the ocean represent the greatest danger to buildings in the vicinity. The strength of these furious winds has been known to knock down walls or blow off roofs during each typhoon season.

The client wanted to build a villa which would also function as a guesthouse for weekend parties in the country. The conditions that had to be addressed were: 1) dealing with the humidity of the site; 2) ensuring the splendid view of the ocean above the tree-tops; 3) mitigating the strong winds.

In lifting the building piloti-style above the ground, the architect immediately solved some of the site's more salient problems: the building is no longer obliged to conform to the steep grade of the land, humidity emanating from the ground does not enter the house and clearer views above the tree-tops are gained.

The villa is composed of two volumes; one is an ellipsoidal sphere housing most of the home's general functions, the other is a rectangular parallelepiped solely for sleeping. Each volume is supported by 6 columns of 30 cm of diameter, on a 3.6 m grid formation. As protection against the wind, the sphere faces the valley in an aerodynamic manner, while the rectangle is shielded by thick tree cover. In both, the main skeleton is steel, and the ellipsoidal cage is shaped by laminated timbers.

The exterior of the ellipsoid is entirely clad in copper plates (t=0.35 mm), a technique for which the project is indebted to the traditional technique of shrine carpenters in Japan. The greenish patina which will accrue over time will serve as protection against the corrosion caused by the high salt content of the seaside air.

As per the client's request, interior surfaces are all painted white. In the sphere particularly, one can experience a certain endless space through voids, as well as one's own unreliable senses for understanding space without corners. This game of perception between architectural space and the human body provides the extraordinary aspect sought by the clients.

Photographs: Hiroyuki Hirai

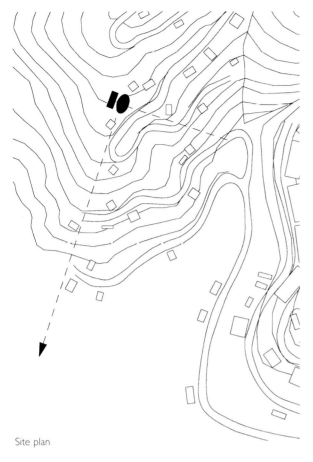

Site plan

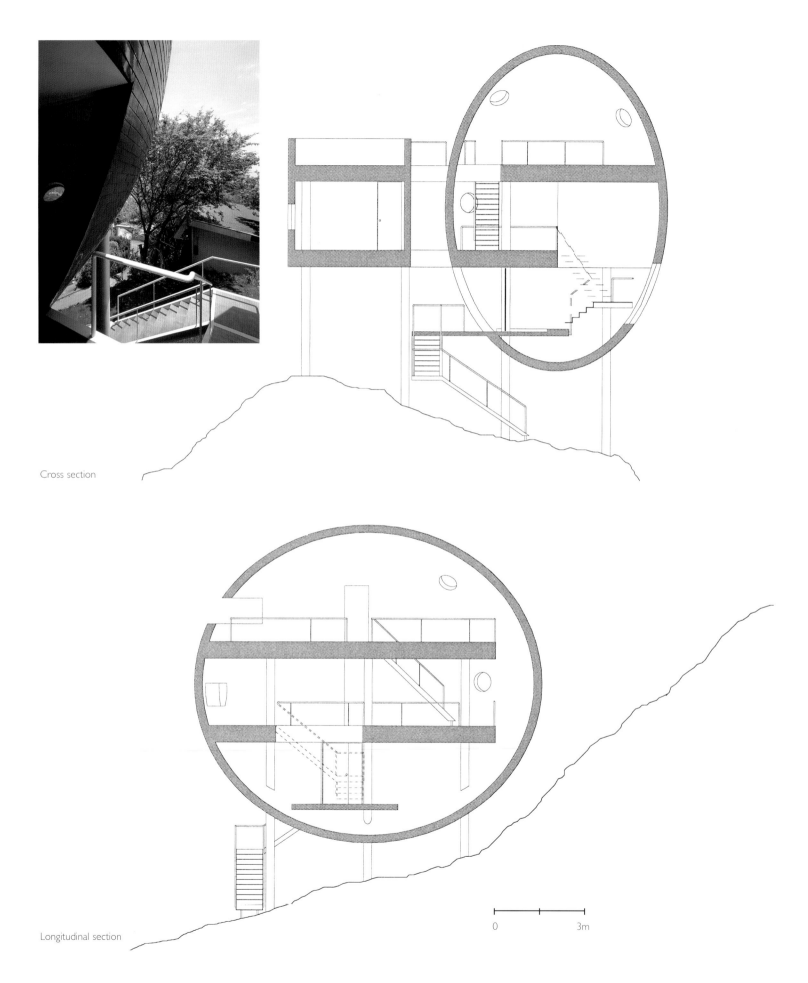

Cross section

Longitudinal section

0   3m

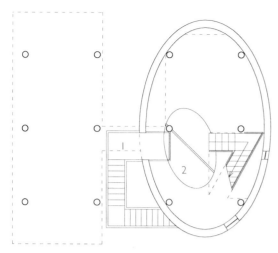

Entrance floor plan

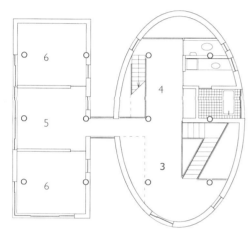

First floor plan

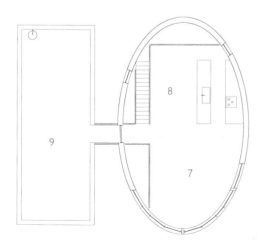

Second floor plan

1. Entrance porch 2. Entrance 3. Hall 4. Gallery
5. Anteroom 6. Bedroom 7. Living room
8. Dining room 9. Roof terrace

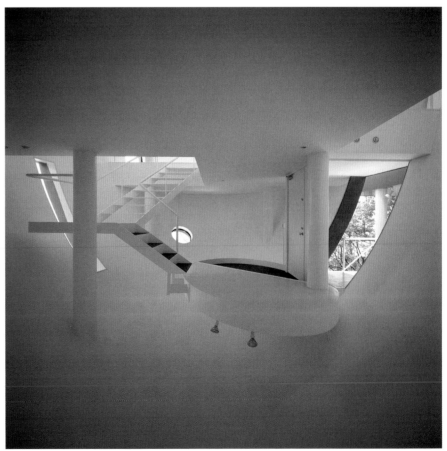

Studio Archea
Abitazione Unifamiliare a Leffe

Val Seriana, Bergamo, Italy

The brief for this project consisted of the replacement of the interior of a historical building in the town of Leffe near the Italian city of Bergamo in the Seriana valley, on a narrow site that was seriously limited by the two adjoining buildings.

The scheme, carried out by the young Italian architects of the Studio Archea group, which is made up of Giovanni Polazzi, Laura Andreini y Marco Casamonti, was based on the total demolition of the existing building and the complete reconstruction, starting from a new foundation plane that made it possible to create an underground level.

Also, the particular conditions of the site and the required distances from the adjoining building, led to the design of facades that were very different from the original ones.

In close contact with the adjoining buildings, the facades are blind, without any type of windows, so the walls appear to be torn by horizontal strips that cause an unusual play of light and shade, both at night and during the day.

The four floors of the dwelling are organized as follows: the ground floor houses the kitchen and the double height dining room; the first floor houses the day area, and the upper floors the night area, which is also subdivided into two levels.

On the other side, in the access area, a large atrium of triple height extends the space vertically and connects all the floors of the house visually, which makes a very fluid architectural promenade through the house's interior.

On the rear facade of the building there is a very narrow space between the new volume and the adjoining buildings. This resulted in the design of a peculiar system of blinds with a structure of stainless steel coated in oxidized copper that occupies the whole surface of the facade facing the valley.

The design of this mobile wall emphasizes the formal motif of the main facade, which is perforated with long narrow openings in the skin of Santa Fiora stone.

On this side of the building the entrance is protected with a large cornice, also clad in copper, which defines the main entrance to the building and casts a large shadow over it, creating a very expressive effect.

Photographs: Alessandro Ciampi, Pietro Savorelli

Rear elevation

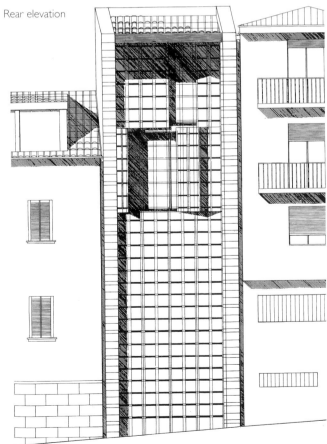

109

The rear facade is characterized by the presence of a
particular system of blinds
with a structure of stainless
steel and a cladding of oxidized copper. The design of
this mobile wall emphasizes
the formal motif of the main
facade, perforated with long
narrow openings.

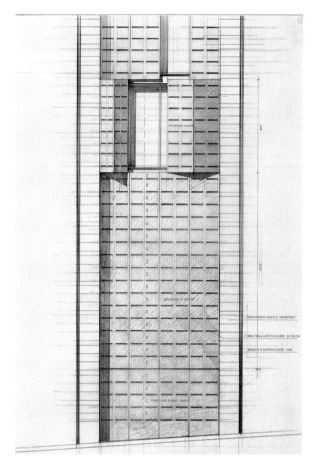

110

Ground floor plan

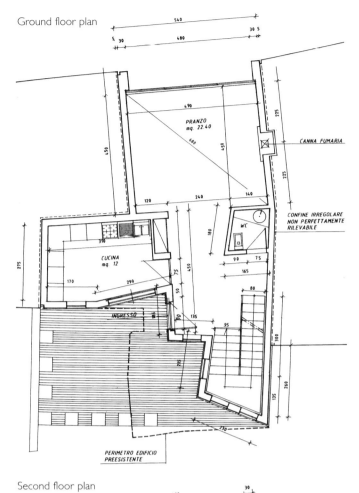

Second floor plan

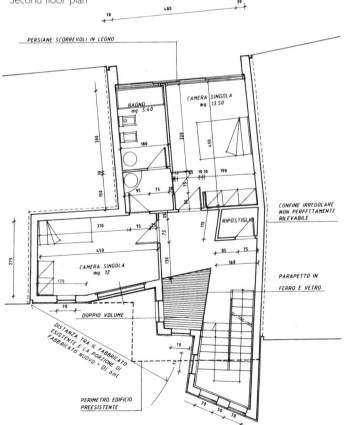

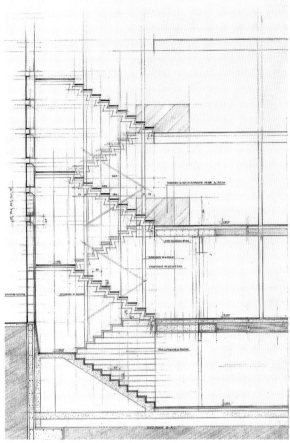

Cross section

The facade, closely related to the adjoining buildings, has no openings. However, it is crossed by beams of light that penetrate through a succession of small fissures in the wall clad in Santa Fiora stone.

A large cornice crowns the construction, casting a generous shadow over the facade.

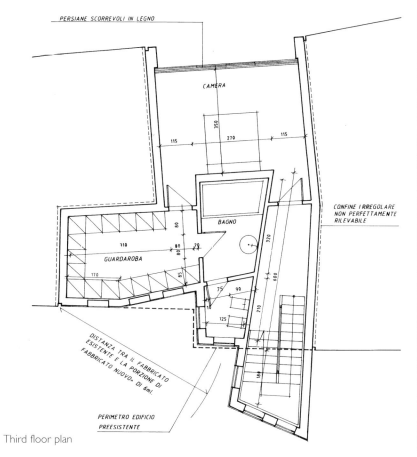

PERSIANE SCORREVOLI IN LEGNO

CAMERA

CONFINE IRREGOLARE
NON PERFETTAMENTE
RILEVABILE

BAGNO

GUARDAROBA

DISTANZA TRA IL FABBRICATO
ESISTENTE E LA PORZIONE DI
FABBRICATO NUOVO> DI 6ml.

PERIMETRO EDIFICIO
PREESISTENTE

Third floor plan

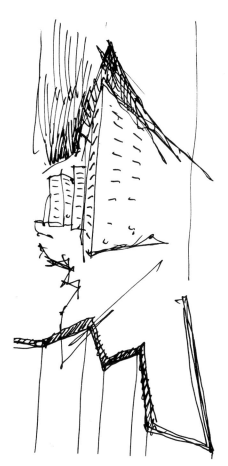

EOK: Eichinger Oder Knechtl
Monocoque, Wohnung Schretter

Vienna, Austria

This former laundry attic room has been converted into a 35 m², fully equiped loft. Apart from the separate 15 m² bedroom, all basic functions are housed in a "multidirectional unit". One wall has been removed and the roof structure has been covered with meral and plasterboard. Additionally, part of the exterior garret wall has been replaced with a large, two-part, movable glass construction.

Inside the heavy metal security door is a large cupboard which acts as a translucent room-divider and houses the washing machine and control unit for all functions, which are operable by remote control. In the evening it transforms into a huge lamp. The lavatory is located at one end of the cupboard, separated by stainless-steel doors that allow access from both sides. These can be closed in front of the lavatory pan so that it disappears into its own storage unit, hidden in a tiny space and leaving a path through the cupboard. Alternatively, a larger, luxurious space can be created.

The path through the cupboard allows access to the kitchen, which is lined by a net wall on one side and the cupboard on the other. Behind the net is the sink, enclosed in a glass cube. The net wall can be folded to create a shower cubicle, its fittings concealed and integrated into a metal column. In the shower area, the black sicaflex gaps in the American oak yacht floor have been routed to form a water drain.

Once the net wall is folded the other way, the shower and sink are concealed, leaving no clue that they exist. It is therefore possible to allow snow to enter the room, creating a unique ambience on certain occasions.

The large, two-part window is electrically operated. Part one tilts upwards until it reaches a height of 2.10 meters. The other part is operated separately and slides outside along the concrete unit, creating a balcony surface that enlarges the size of the room.

Photographs: Margherita Spiluttini; eok

Floor plan

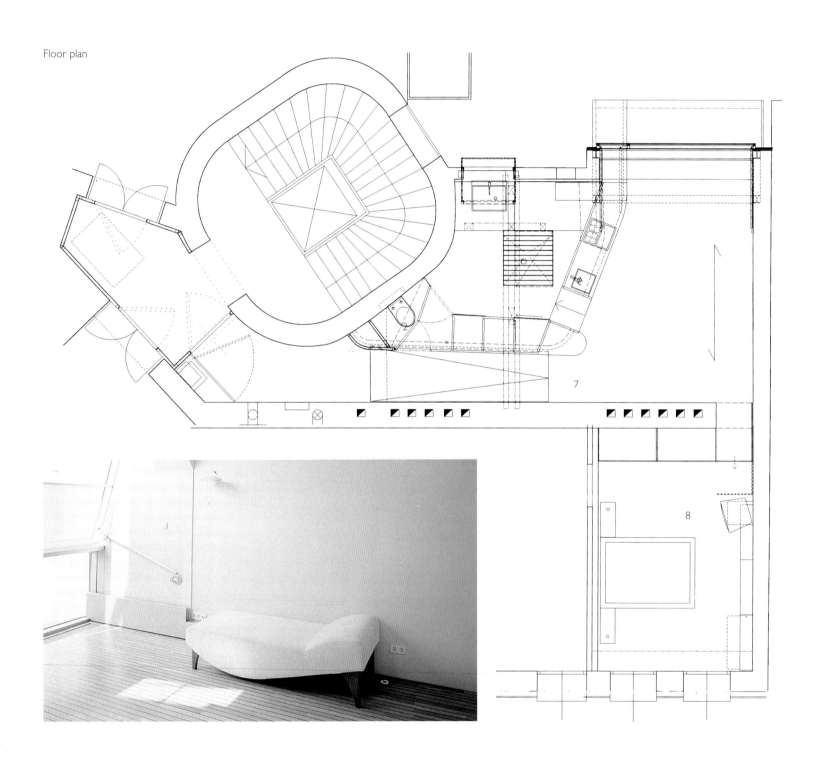

7

8

Sliding window section

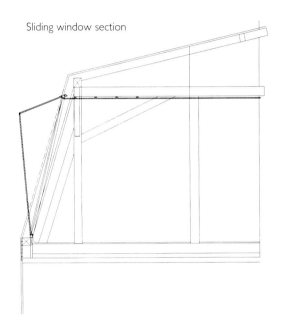

Tilting window section

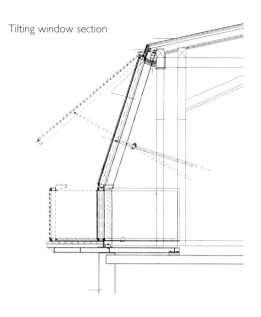

Sliding window detail

Tilting window detail

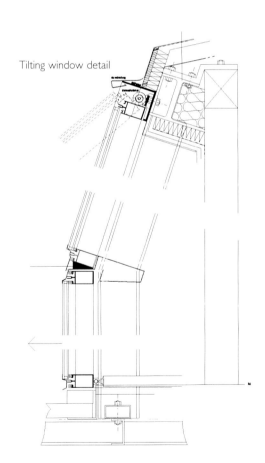

Window elevation

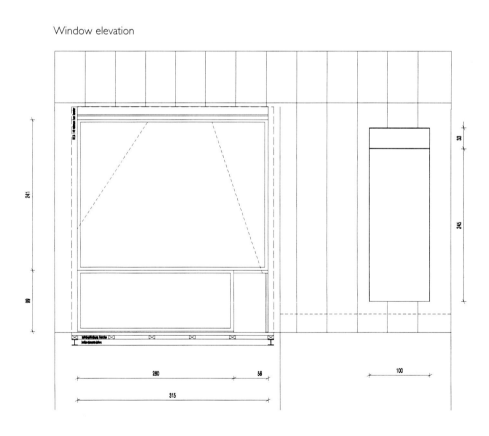

117

Shigeru Ban
Paper House

Yamanakako, Japan

Shigeru Ban has been studying the characteristics of paper as a building element since the eighties. Though there is some resistance to its use in a structural system, paper is a material that may be treated (like wood) to make it resistant to fire, water and damp. It is also easy to recycle and economic. This allowed the architect to work with this element in designs that required speed and low cost, such as the pavilions for refugees from Ruanda and the provisional buildings to house the victims of the Kobe earthquake.

In this scheme, a dwelling of 110 m², the structure is formed by two square horizontal planes with a side of 10 meters and paper tubes aligned in an S-shape with a height of 2.7 meters, a diameter of 280 mm and a thickness of 15 mm. These tubes support the house and defined its different functional spaces, relating them to the surrounding landscape. Ten of these tubes support the vertical loads and eighty interior tubes support the lateral loads. The circle formed by these eighty tubes defines the living room, whereas the circle formed by the square defines the bathroom of the dwelling.

The separation from the exterior is created using a glass wall that may open or close and that can also be covered by canvas curtains to provide privacy and good insulation.

The spatial continuity between the interiors and the landscape is achieved through the horizontal elements and the use of very diaphanous joinery, and through the definition of the interior spaces with the minimum number of elements, following the example of the great architects of Modernism.

The paper tubes also allow the spaces defined to maintain a very subtle relation with the surrounding spaces, letting in the light and views between them.

Photographs: Hiroyuki Hirai

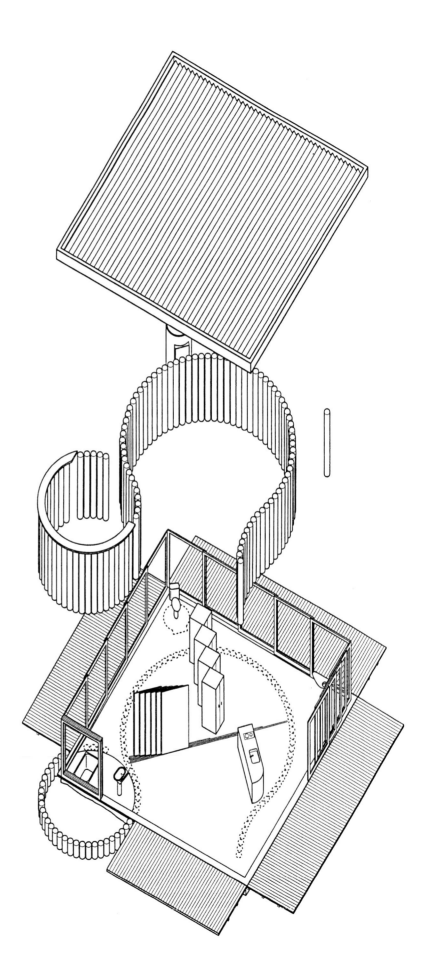

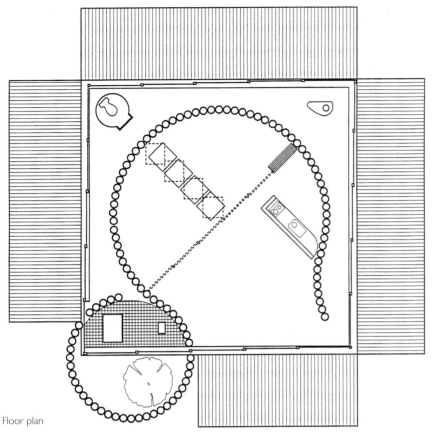

Floor plan

Section

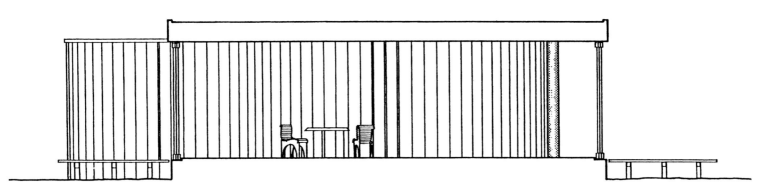

The relation between the interior and exterior spaces is a constant in the designs of Shigeru Ban. In this scheme, the enormous glazed window can be opened to leave the dwelling totally open to the exterior. To emphasize this relation even further, overhanging terraces were created to extend the floor area and bring the dwelling closer to nature.

Robert Oshatz
Gibson Boathouse/Studio

Lake Oswego, Oregon. USA

The Gibson's had an existing boathouse but felt it was a blemish on their property. They wanted to reuse the existing boat stall but build a new boathouse while adding a new studio and study. The site went from the lake up the hillside to the driveway above. Since the driveway to their property is shared with neighbors, it was decided to build the studio into the hillside and have a sod roof so the structure would not be noticed as the neighbor drove down -the driveway. Mrs. Gibson, an artist, wanted her studio space to have high ceilings and ample natural light. Mr. Gibson, an entrepreneur, wanted a more intimate space to keep track of his business activities. The structure grows out of stone walls that are shared by an arching sod roof. The roof is constructed with straight Douglas fir glue-laminated beams and fir decking.

Photographs: Robert Oshatz

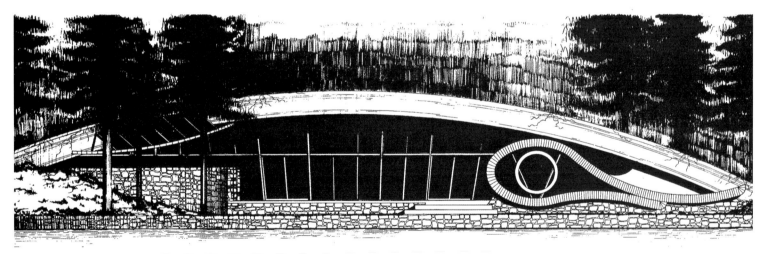

Floor plan
1. Entry walk 2. Storage 3. Toilet 4. Study 5. Vault 6. Lake Oswego 7. Boathouse

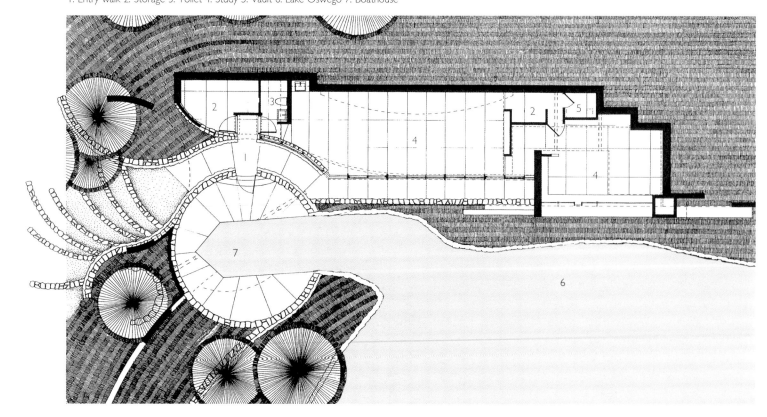

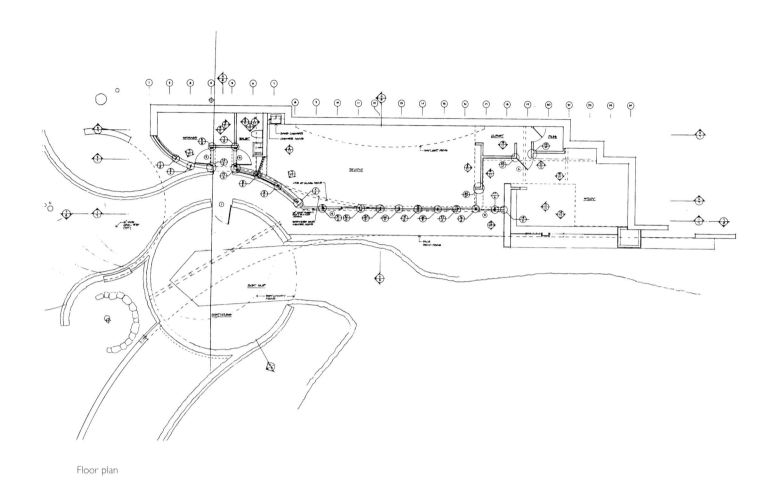

Floor plan

The idea of building a studio in the jetty area added a privileged space to the dwelling. It is camouflaged by the vegetation-covered roof, which hides it from the passers-by who use the path leading to the other houses.

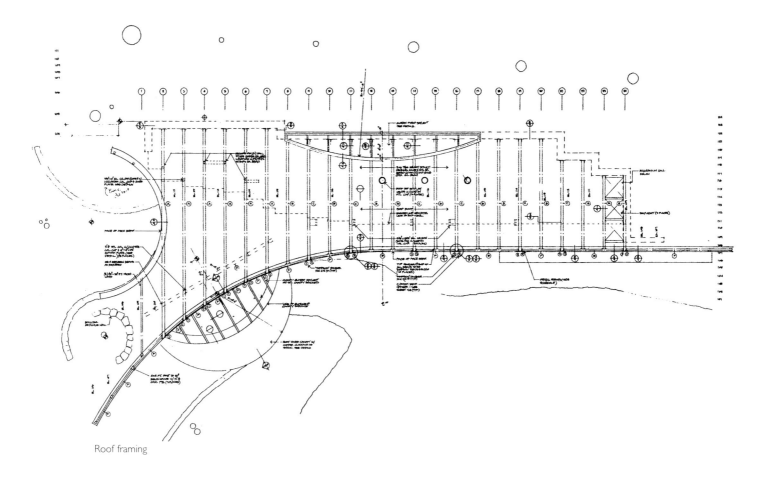

Roof framing

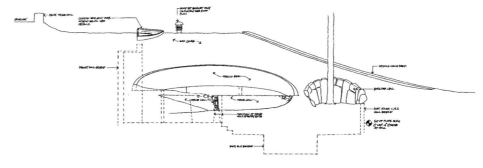

South-west section

The main elements used in this scheme - stone, wood and grass- are completely eco-logical and maintain a pleasant relationship with the surroundings of the studio-jetty. A small skylight in the vegetation-covered roof provides toplighting for the interior of the studio.

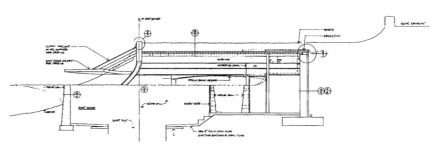

Section

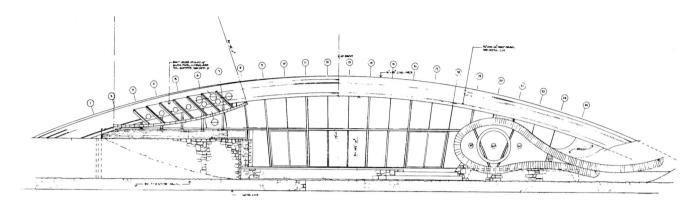

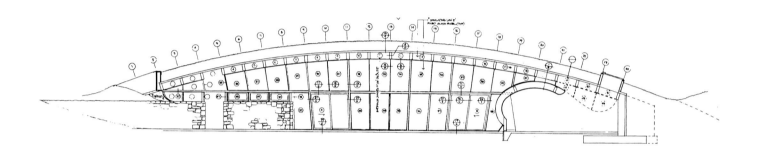

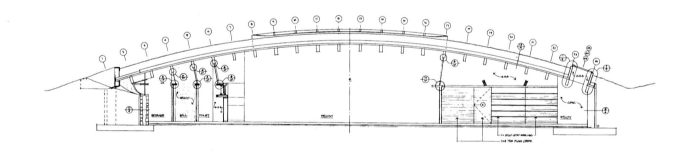

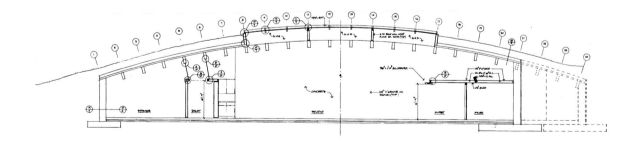

132

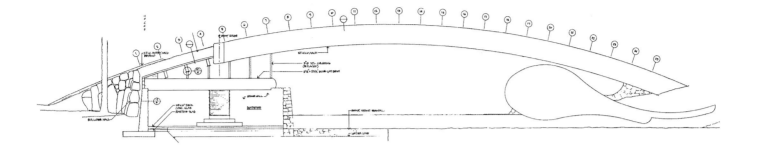

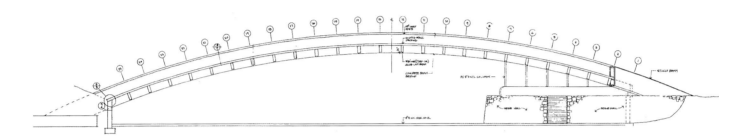

Sections

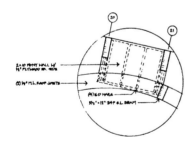

Pony wall from arch to roof

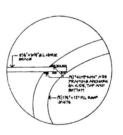

Transom to arch detail

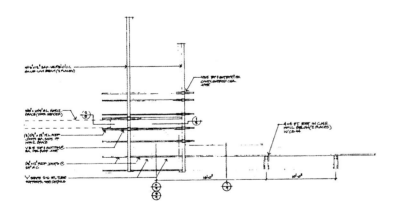

Study roof frame plan

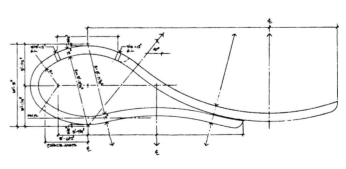

Study arch frame detail

Fabienne Couvert & Guillaume Terver
Villa Ganem

Montrouge, France

This project consisted of an extension of an early twentieth century dwelling situated on a 5810 ft² plot, covered in chestnut trees, lime trees and lilacs. The design called for a damp-resistant pinewood structure covered in varnished oak plywood panels. Two assembly systems were used in order to differentiate the two enlarged volumes: panels with bare joints for the living spaces (bedrooms and sitting room) and panels with covered joints in the building designed for study.

The carpentry, consisting of French-style openings with doors and fixed gaps, is of a fine, imported wood, while the roof was built of zinc sheets. The façade facing the garden can be opened or closed through the use of a series of shutters with a wooden framework and oak slats. These systems of concealment are arranged laterally along the facade. The bulk of the dwelling is a space oriented to benefit from an immense opening toward the garden. Light for the complex is provided by a glazed impost located above the entrance door and a large window to the right of the stairway between the extension and the pavilion.

The extension serves as both distribution area and entranceway. The door, barely visible from the inside, has been finished with wood in order to achieve continuity along the interior wall faces. The studio resembles a block, with interior shutters hanging above the volumes facing the garden and the large windows. It is accessed by means of a wooden staircase lying on the axis formed by the pavilion's load-bearing wall and the enlargement's load-bearing wall, is like a block. A banquet table keeps the shutters in place and protects them from the void. The loft's surface and the shutters are made of varnished plywood panels. The studio is a 15-foot-high volume and is accessed from three sectors of the house: from the pavilion; by crossing a private area housing the shower and wardrobe; from the sitting room by means of a sliding door, and from the garden through a large opening. The space also benefits from four sources of natural light: a skylight in the pavilion, a horizontal, south-facing opening, an opening above the garden on the west side and a high, fixed opening on the east. Inscribed onto the back of the existing building, the new structure is protected from the street and opens entirely onto the garden. In order to maintain a perfect interpretation of the existing structure and to achieve an evolving integration into its surroundings, the architect has opted for an irregular geometrical scheme, a break from the existing shape. This differentiation between the volumes corresponds to a disassociation of programs.

Photographs: G. Terver; X. Lewis

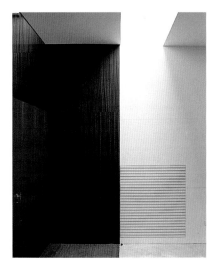
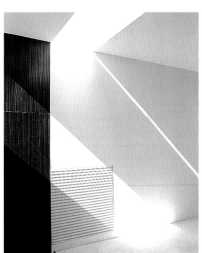

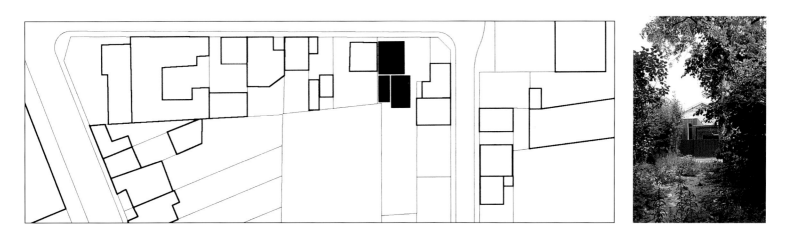

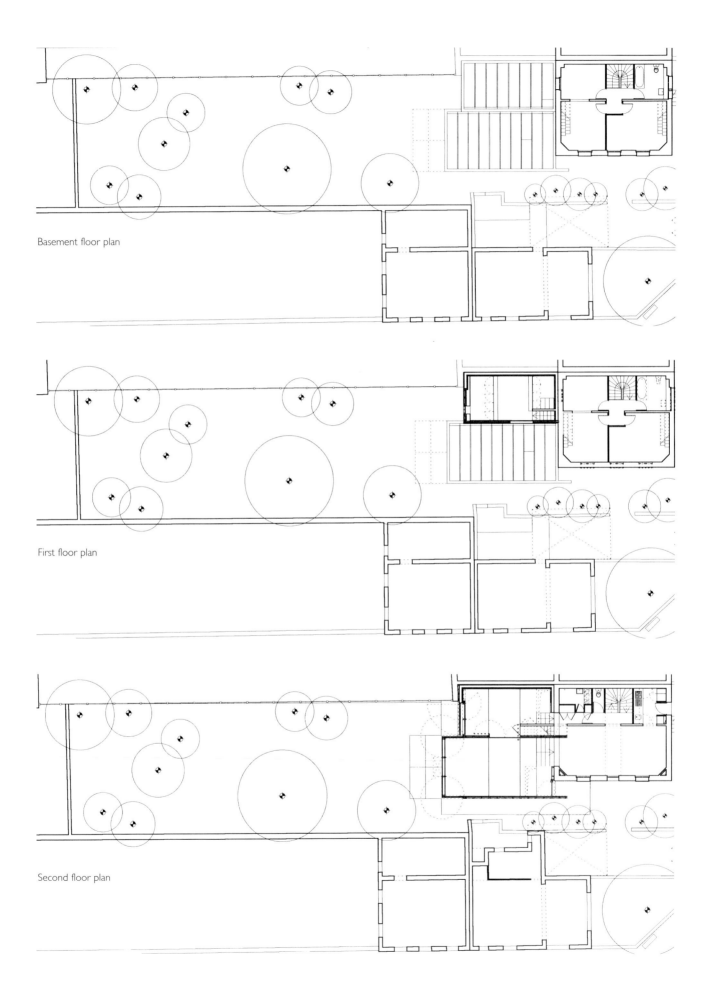

Basement floor plan

First floor plan

Second floor plan

138

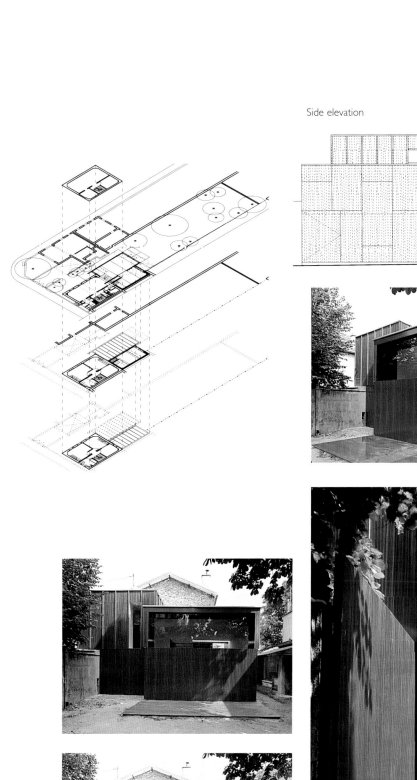

Side elevation

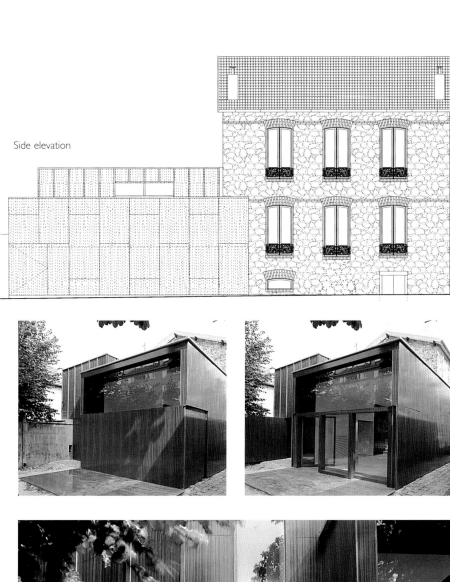

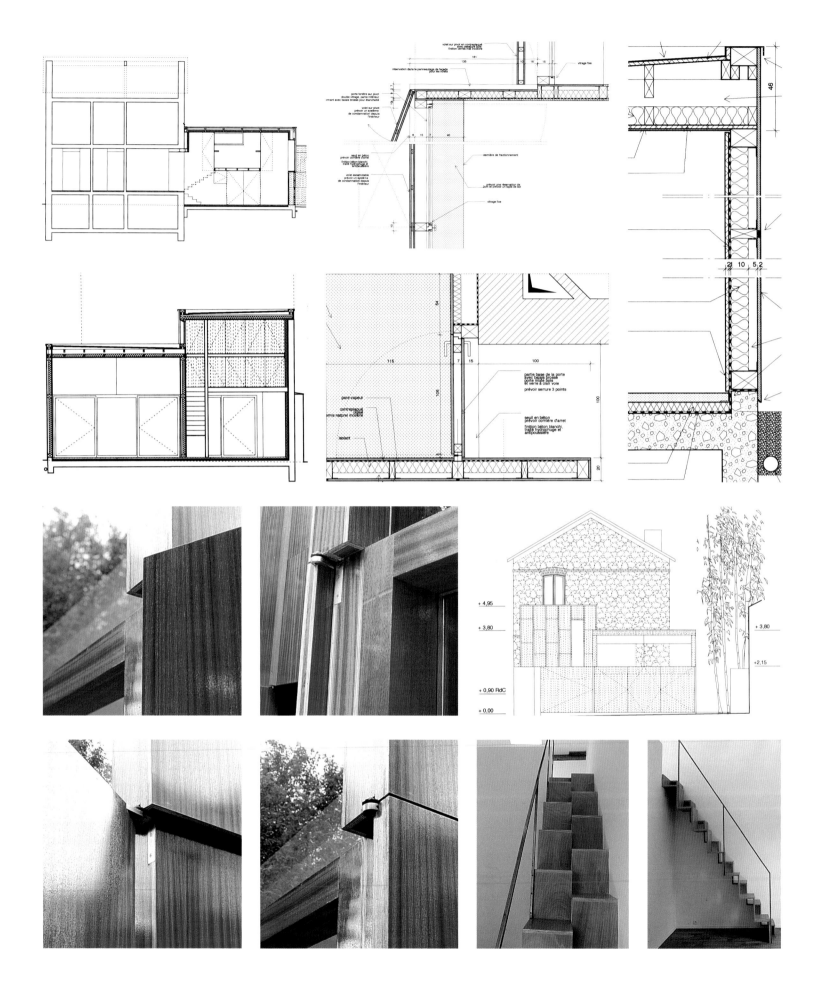

140

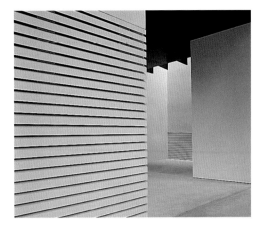
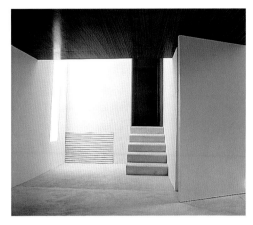
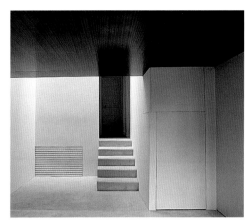

The doors, hardly visible from the interior, have been finished in exotic wood in order to maintain the continuity of the wall surfaces. The staircase which leads to the studio is contained within the axis of the pavilion's load bearing wall and the extension's load bearing wall.

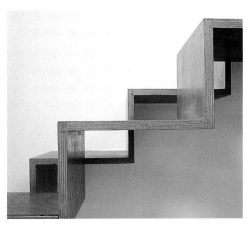

Philip Gumuchdjian
D.P. Think Tank / Boathouse

Skibbereen, County Cork. Ireland

Set into the River Ilen in west Ireland, the building was conceived as a retreat for a famous film producer.

The architecture reflects a wide range of references: boathouse structures, barns, cow sheds, chalets, and a European perspective on Japanese pavilions. The building resolves these references into a simple expression of frame, roof and screens.

The dominant element of the design is the overhanging roof structure, which provides physical and psychological protection from the considerable annual rainfall.

A clear hierarchy of architectural elements (roof, structure, screens and glazing) was crucial to creating its legibility as an apparently enclosed "found" structure - a simple and timeless object. Transparency and perforated screens were deployed to keep the building open to the elements but also frame views and suggest enclosure and protection.

The materials of the structure are selected to juxtapose "stable" elements such as glass and stainless steel against the highly "changeable" and weathering materials of the cedar roof planks, slats and decks and the iroko frame. Set against the vivid colors and reflections of the site -green fields, blue/silver river, dramatic blues and grays of the sky- the silver of the building permanently changes color when the roof and structural frame get wet during showers and bleached under the sunshine.

Photographs: W. Hutchmacher / ARTUR

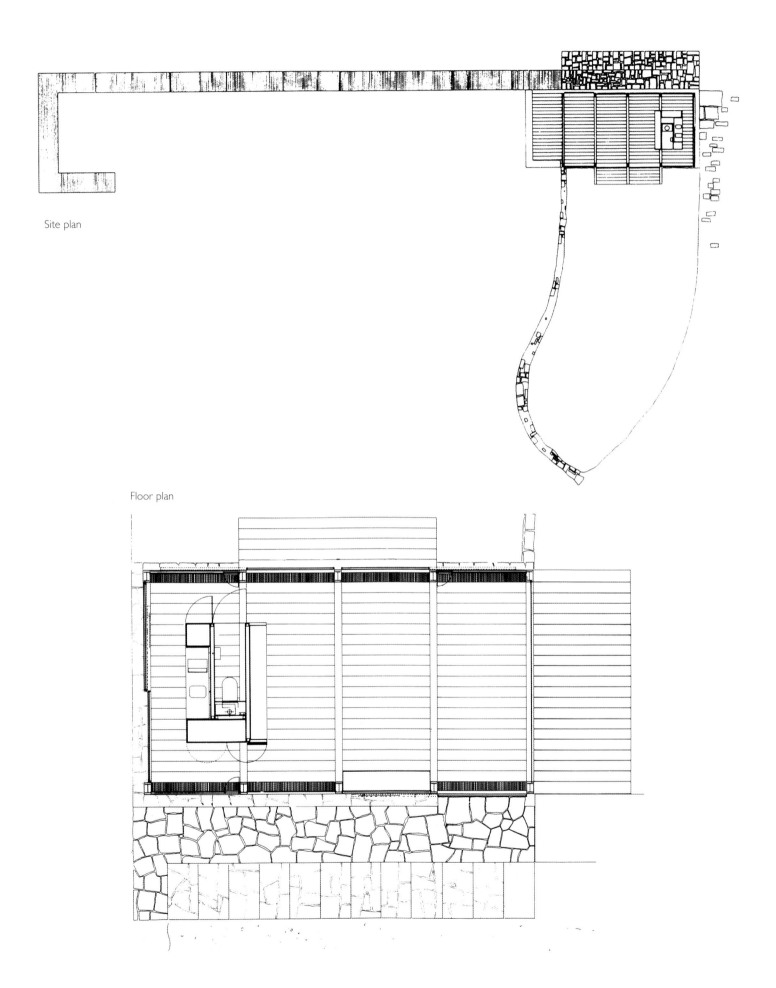

Site plan

Floor plan

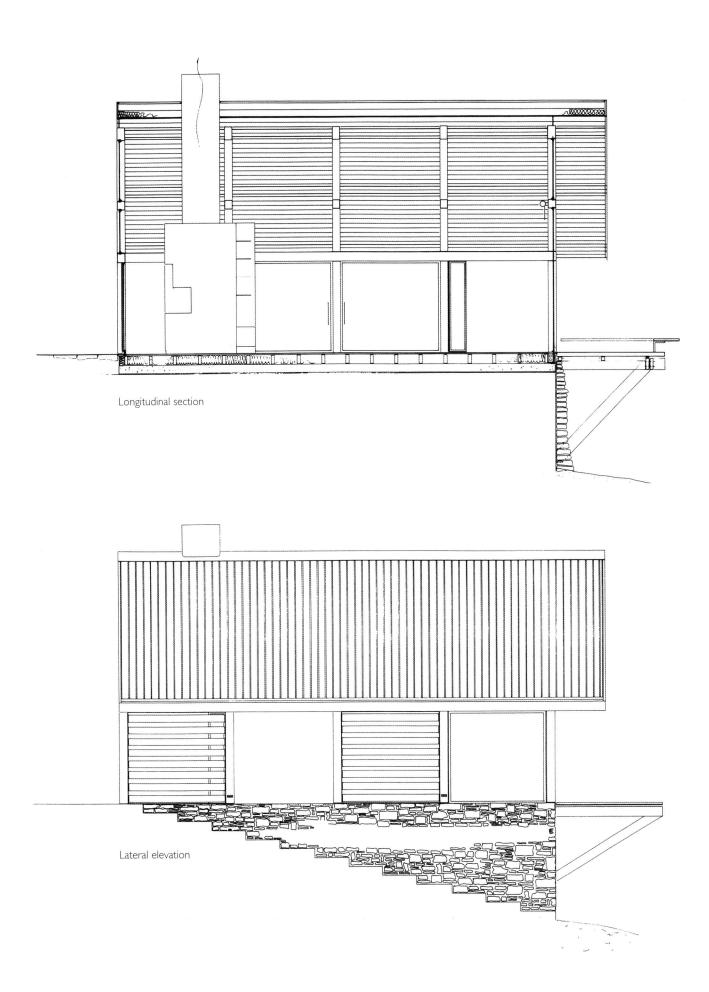

Longitudinal section

Lateral elevation

A long pier extends the house onto the river, creating a space for escape and a perspective from which the interior of the dwelling can be appreciated.

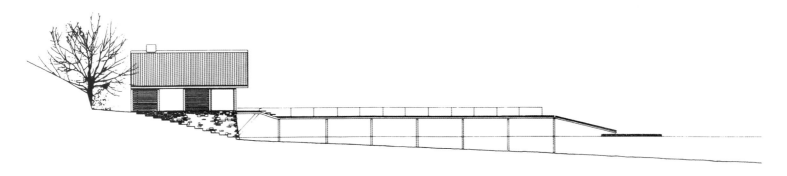

Elevations

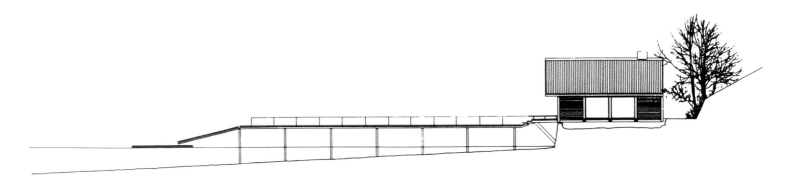

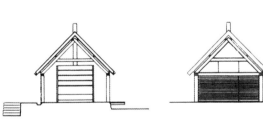

Cross section

Rear elevation

Main elevation

Will Bruder
Byrne Residence

North Scottsdale, Arizona, USA

The sculptural design concept of this residence was to create a metaphorical series of abstract canyon walls of concrete masonry, emerging like geological landmarks from the home's natural desert site. As such, the home's architectural concrete masonry and metal-clad frame walls embrace the residence's main entrance, as well as its living and circulation/gallery spaces. Furthermore, these walls highlight the angular geometry of the building's plan as it grows from the asymmetrical, tapering alignments of the canyon walls. These elements in turn visually extend the design out into the undisturbed natural desert site, creating interesting outdoor living spaces and courtyards.

The house is incorporated into the natural slope of the site's north-east corner, allowing the building's basic functional needs to develop on two levels. As it is placed on the site, the lower level is buried into the grade with a primarily south-western view exposure. The angular orientation of the structure, running parallel to the natural site contours, enhances the relationship with the terrain, while optimizing the distant view opportunities of all the living spaces on the main level. The tilted and leaning orientation of the masonry canyon walls serves to dramatically frame the site's distant desert vistas as one moves though the structure.

Only simple concrete block walls, treated as a dynamic sculptural element, could capture the potential of this architectural concept. Laid at a three-degree slope from the horizontal concrete foundations and leaning at varying angles from vertical, the beautifully crafted masonry walls are ever-changing in the desert sun. With the daily and seasonal variations of shadows playing off the subtle coursing offsets together with the buff-colored masonry and the angular alignments of the plan's geometry, the architecture possesses a mysterious quietness and power in the landscape. With a view to maximize these effects, the main roof is raised 4" above the supporting wall by skylit sculptural steel brackets which allow the sun to energize the interior as well.

Carefully balanced by vertical walls of masonry, metal and glass, the house exists as a poem of particular invention and originality. To complement the contrast with the dominant concrete masonry wall of the design scheme, wall and fascia elements are clad in blue/blackened copper and acid-etched galvanized metal. These materials, with their purple/bronze and pewter hues, will blend well with the natural landscape and the buff CMU.

Completing the exterior palette is a glazing of clear and "solex" green non-reflective glass, set in custom configuration and details. The scale, sculptural form and the simplicity of its materials make the Byrne Residence an organic architectural statement that blends with and enhances its unique desert setting.

Photographs: Bill Timmerman

Upper level plan

Lower level plan

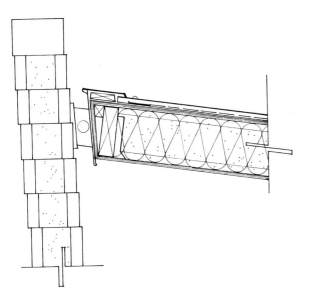

Construction detail of intersection between the wall and the roof.

Given the characteristics of the site of the dwelling, a desert landscape in Arizona, it was fundamental to achieve a complete mastery of natural light. It was not a question, as in other cases, of maximizing the light but of being able to graduate it according to the needs of the inhabitants. The careful placing of the windows and an emphasis on top lighting transform the interior of the dwelling into a very intimate and welcoming space.

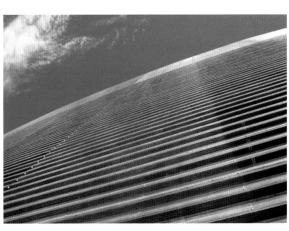

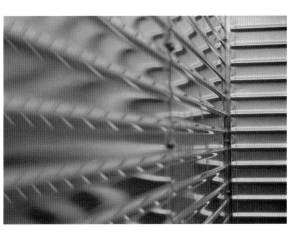

Koen van Velsen
Vos Family House

Amsterdam, The Netherlands

The Vos House, designed by the firm of Koen van Velsen, is located on the Island of Borneo in the port of Amsterdam, opposite a canal. It is a narrow terraced house whose impressive facade distinguishes it from the surrounding buildings. The facade has been solved as a screen that allows an "urban garden" to be created in the part of the dwelling that opens onto the street. This is an imaginative and innovative approach, since it breaks with the traditional idea of the back garden; each floor has an interior terrace that opens onto the street.

The scheme is distributed on three floors. The ground floor houses the garage, from which the dwelling is accessed by means of a staircase. Glass walls separate the interior of the house from the terrace that gives onto the street behind the screen, whose glazed windows let natural light into the interior. A large tree stands in the inner courtyard, rising through the different floors of the dwelling in its vertical progression.

The organization of the dwelling spaces is another example of the architect's audacity. The most spectacular feature is the design of the kitchen and dining room. A wall separates these two spaces and acts as a storage space on the kitchen side.

The particularity of this wall is that it is mobile and allows the kitchen to be made larger or smaller according to the needs. Versatility was one of the requirements of the client, who wanted a flexible dwelling that could adapt to changes.

Chromatic uniformity is a feature of the whole dwelling, with flat polished surfaces. The spaces are separated by walls that act as storage spaces and maintain order in the dwelling. The space is bright and sober, flooded with natural light through all the windows and through the skylights located on the top floor.

Photographs: Duccio Malagamba

Basement plan

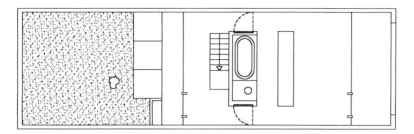

Ground floor plan

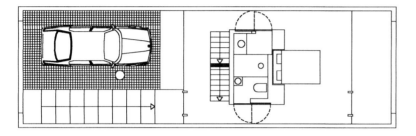

First floor plan

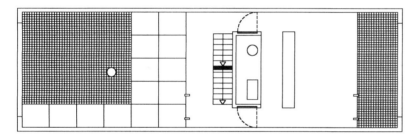

Second floor plan

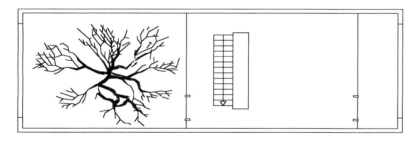

Roof floor plan

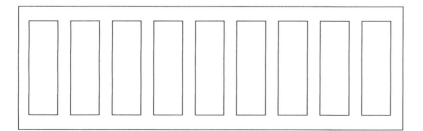

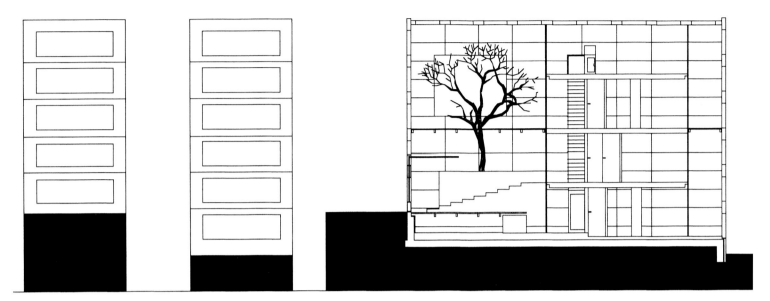

Elevations   Longitudinal section

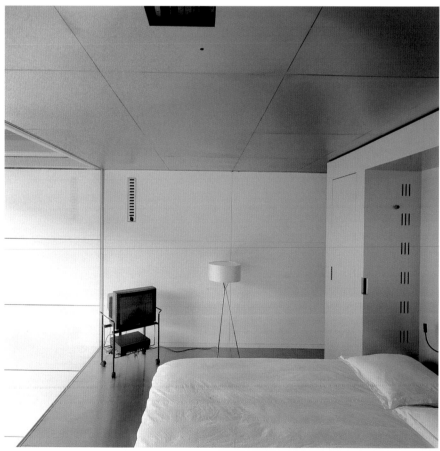

Takao Shiotsuka
Shigemi House

Oita, Japan

Various factors and considerations came into play when determining the final form that this house would take. Its unusual shape was developed for specific reasons.

First was the wish to protect the façades, which are clad in wooden boards, from the rain. Another was to create the feeling of a spacious interior without actually increasing the ground space available. Additionally, continuity with the landscape was a goal. The access road slopes up toward the house, the embankment falls away on one side and rises on the other. So instead of standardized 90° angles, the architects instead opted for sloped façades.

The clients run a timber company and wished to fill the home, inside and out, with their company's product. Their original suggestion was to create wide eaves as a necessity for protecting the fine wood of the façades from the elements.

Instead, the architects proposed tilting the perimeter walls outward, thus creating a unified shape that fulfilled the function of eaves. This exterior treatment has the additional advantage of broadening perspectives within the home as well. The total area of the ceiling is 130 m², while that of the floor space is 100 m².

Photographs: Kaori Ichikawa

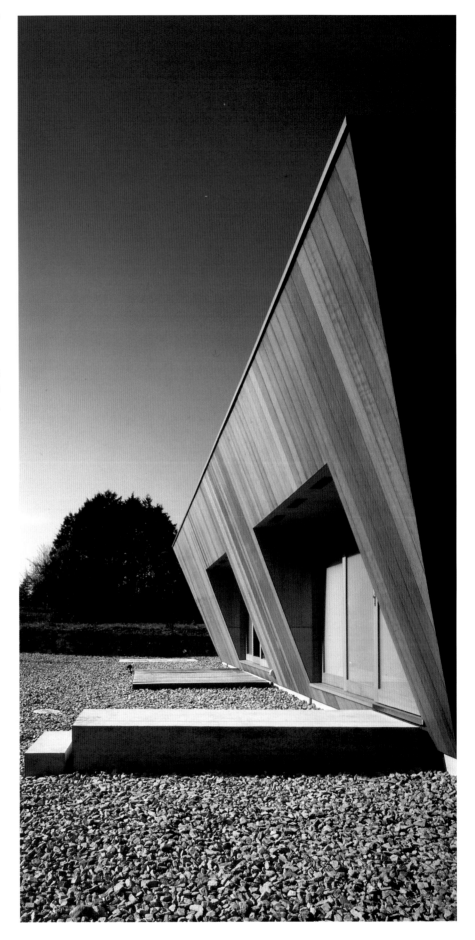

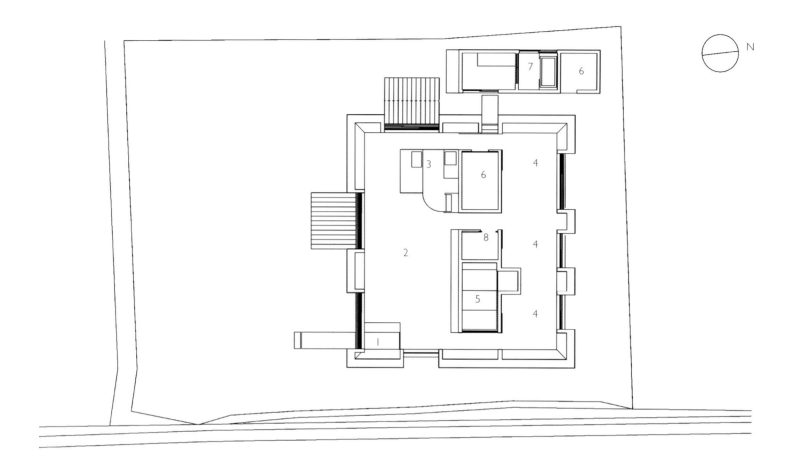

1. Entrance
2. Living room
3. Kitchen
4. Bedroom
5. Japanese tatami room
6. Storage
7. Bathroom
8. Lavatory

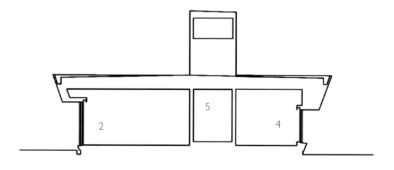

Sections

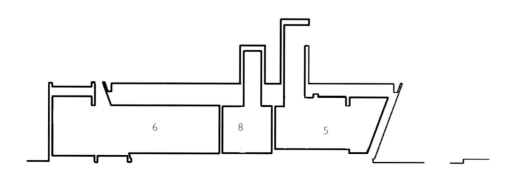

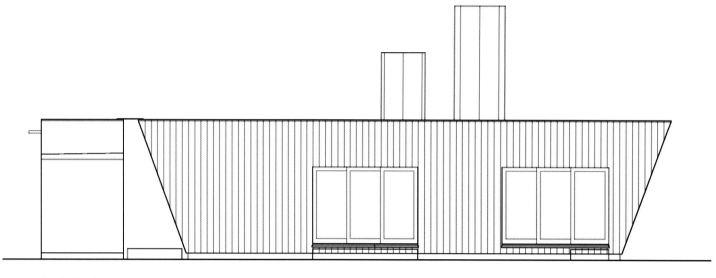

South elevation

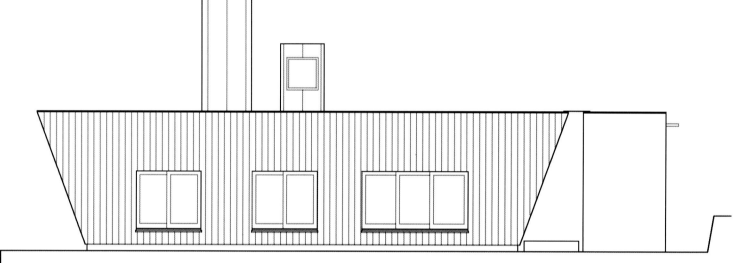

North elevation

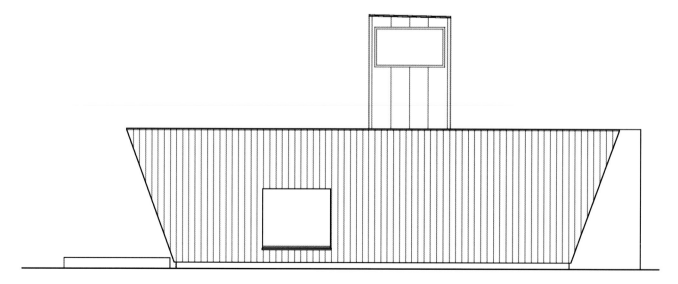

East elevation

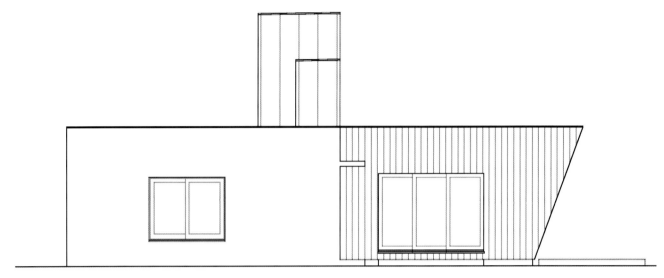

West elevation

Morger & Degelo Architekten
Nadolny House

Dornach, Switzerland

In the far south of the urban environment of Basel is situated the village Dornach. Among other family houses, slightly elevated from a small crossroads, the light and compact cedar wood house is standing on a terrace. The disposition of plan and elevation is determined by the open view to the south on one hand, and the restricting neighborhood to the north on the other. While the north-oriented entrance side allows hardly any outlooks and the lateral windows only selective ones, the southern front with its wide glazed surface is opened up.

Only an efficient modular wood construction enables such a tremendous contrast of the undividedly flowing living room on the ground floor and the various private rooms, separated by sliding wall elements, on the upper floor. The load is transmitted to the outer walls, to the glued wall elements as well as to the massive, dark blue window frame of the airing casement. Its static purpose goes with its intention of design, stressing its plasticity in opposition to unremovable glass. Therefore only the actual openings —the airing casements— are to be noticed, while the permanent glass, functioning as outlook and light opening, is part of the outer membrane, frameless and flush.

Photographs: Ruedi Walti

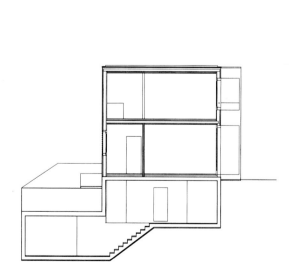

Basement floor plan

Ground floor plan

First floor plan

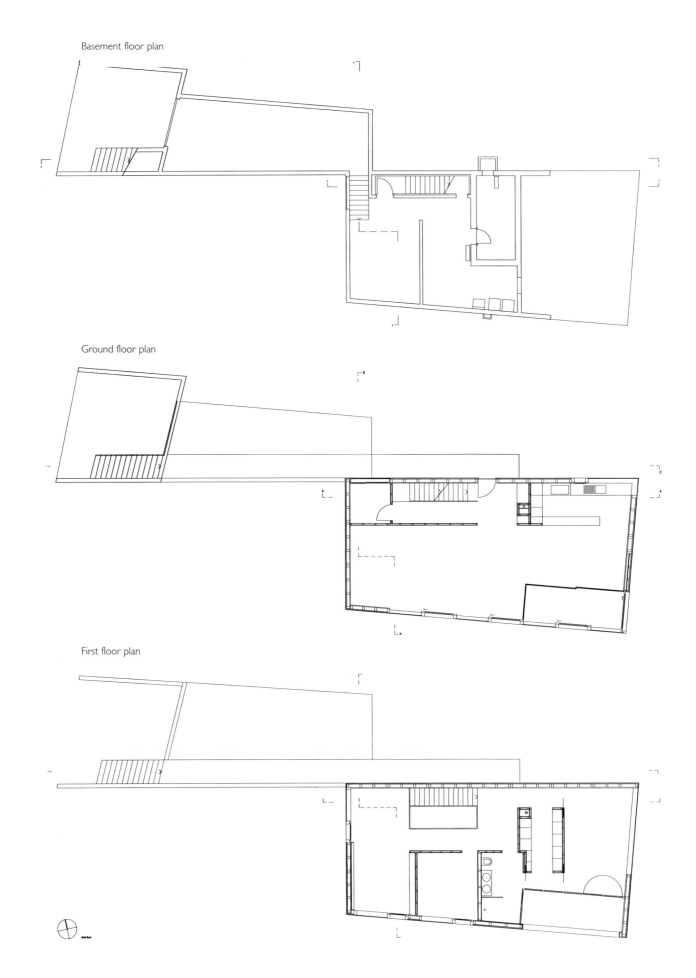

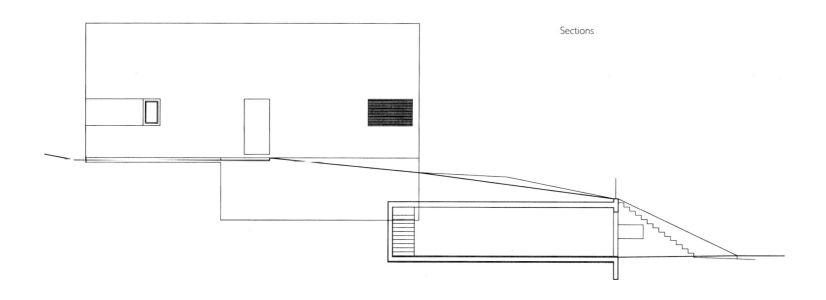

Sections

Ventilation construction detail

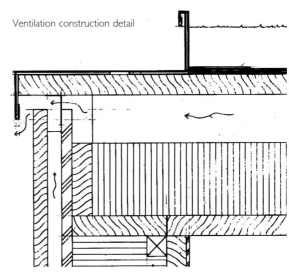

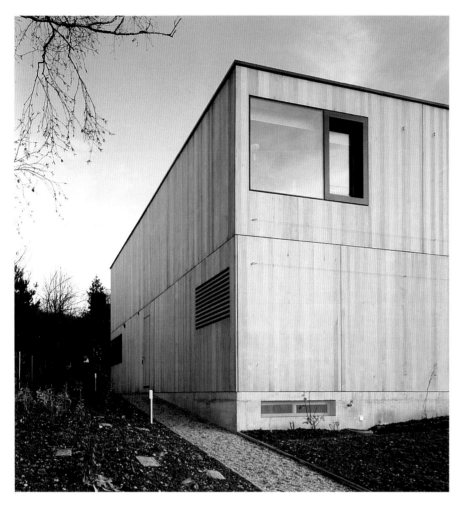

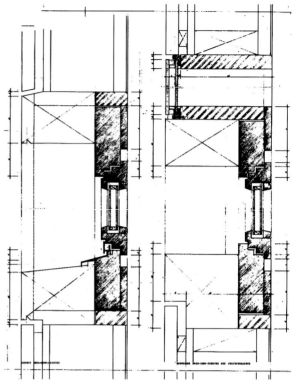

Window construction details

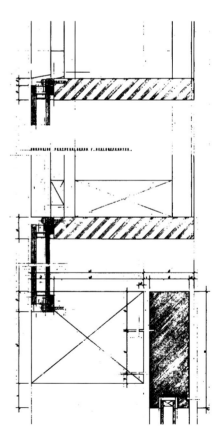

176

Shin Takamatsu & Associates
Iwai House

Minami-ku, Japan

Alone in open fields on the edge of town, in an almost defenseless site beyond an industrial belt, stands this two-story private house, built in reinforced concrete and partly steel frame. On both interior and exterior, the architects have brought to bear all the expressive potential of concrete.

The most noticeable feature of the exterior is the curved wall to the left of the entrance on the main facade. Traditionally in architecture, the wall divides inside and out, yet here the curve gradually draws visitors inside and deepens the ambiguity of the relationship between the two. At first glance this convex wall seems rather aggressive, but within the residence its concavity becomes intimate.

The curved wall also forms the outer edge of a secluded courtyard, and incorporates a raised walkway and a terrace from which one can contemplate the scenery. The courtyard and the large windows overlooking it are protected by a brise-soleil.

The glazed entrance hall leads into a sinuous corridor in which the untreated structural concrete creates a fine visual balance with the wooden flooring. Concrete is left unadorned throughout much of the house, for example in the columns, and complements the plastered surfaces, largely in white with patches of primary colors.

Although the house is thoroughly modern, the interior owes a great deal of its delicacy to traditional Japanese aesthetics. The atrium leading to the terrace is a good example of the common ground that exists between the two approaches.

Photographs: Nacása & Partners

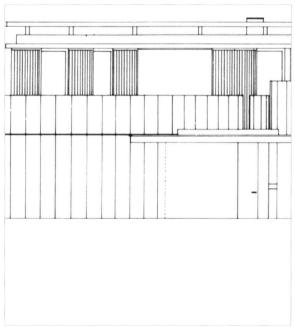

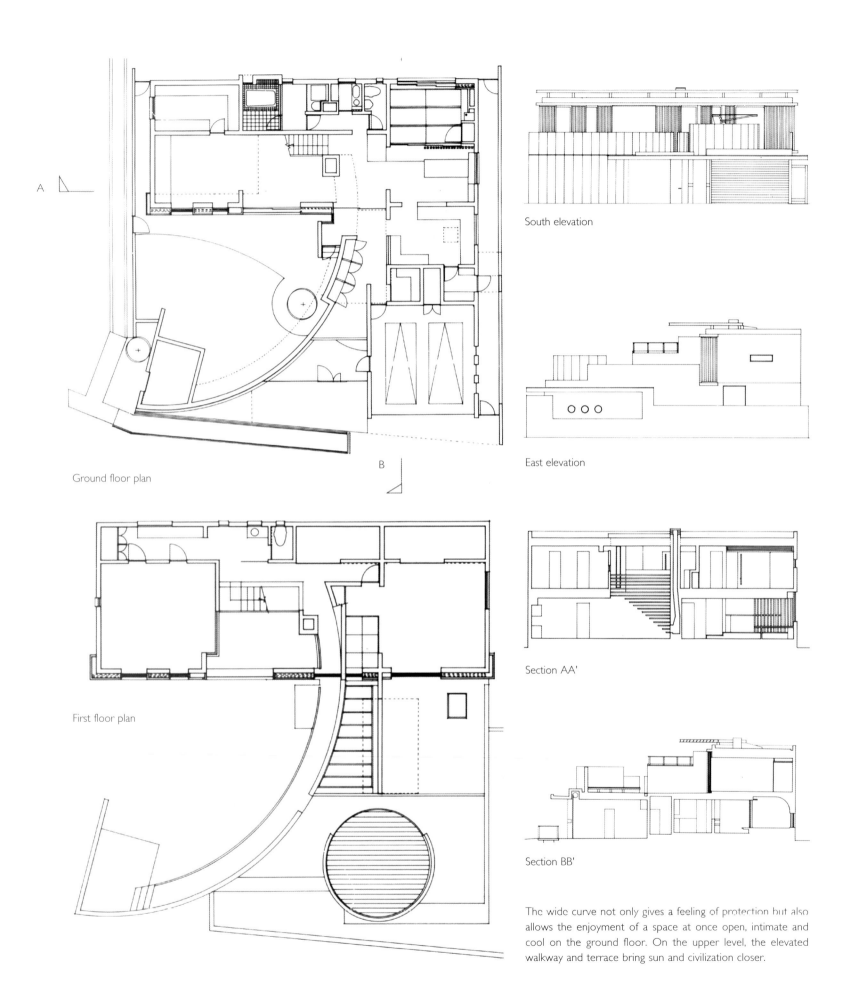

Ground floor plan

A

B

South elevation

East elevation

First floor plan

Section AA'

Section BB'

The wide curve not only gives a feeling of protection but also allows the enjoyment of a space at once open, intimate and cool on the ground floor. On the upper level, the elevated walkway and terrace bring sun and civilization closer.

Augustin + Frank
Viesel House

Falkensee, Germany

The project is situated outside of Berlin's city borders. Many of the inhabitants of Berlin nowadays move to the outskirts in search of a closer affinity to nature and with the desire to have their own house. This is also such a case. Nevertheless, this project has an unusual background and an unusual program. The clients, a married couple, run an antiquarian bookshop. The main turnover is made online, and for this reason they have decided to close the shop and move, with all the books, into the countryside. The program for this building includes living space and workspace for two persons, and the room for 370 running meters of books. In order to realize this project the architects planned a house, which is 18 meters in length, an in breadth 6 meters on the ground floor and 7.5 in the upper story. The books are kept mainly in the upper story. The house does not have a cellar because the ground-water level is high, and a raised ground floor level was not desired. The ground floor holds the weight of the whole book collection and is therefore solidly built using masonry and concrete. The upper story has been built over this, using a light timber frame construction. This separation has led to the house being able to be built very quickly. Whilst the ground floor was developed at the site itself, the upper story and windows were prefabricated in the workshop. In comparison with the surrounding buildings, the volume of the house is very large. In order to compensate for this the architects have drawn it out lengthways, similar to the shape of the plot itself. In this manner the house can get small garden and street elevations. From these sides, it is only possible to guess at the length to which the building stretches back. The large window openings are also on these sides. From the neighboring plots, the building appears more closed. The lengthy outer wall, however, does not present itself a homogeneous surface but rather is broken up by the effect of light and shade and by the filter of an open spaced larch boarding. With the exception of the wall at the entrance, which is set back, and of several reinforced concrete parts, all the exterior parts of the building are painted, or emulsified, with one color. The color is monochrome, and therefore the contrast between the fine details and the clear, simple contours of the building are accentuated. The building is situated at the intersection between town and countryside and should therefore contain elements of both. However, it should serve the purpose of familiarizing the occupants -former town-dwellers- with the country lifestyle.

In this case, the most important element is the projecting upper story. By use of this simple method, a space is created which serves a variety of purposes: a protected entrance, an anteroom leading to the kitchen and a space for outdoor activities which is protected from the rain.

Photographs: W. Huthmacher/ARTUR

Site plan

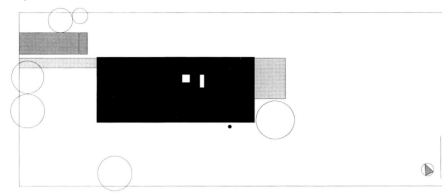

Longitudinal section

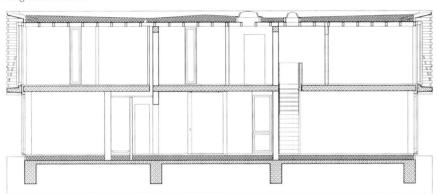

Cross section

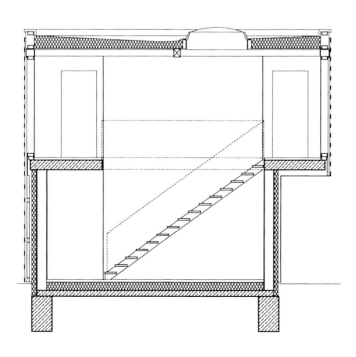

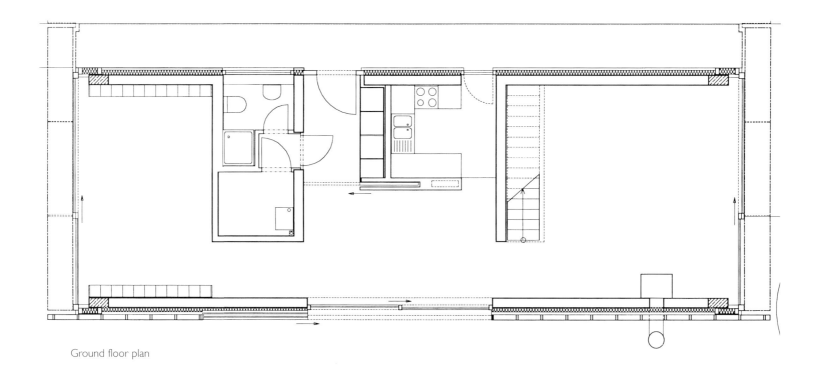

Ground floor plan

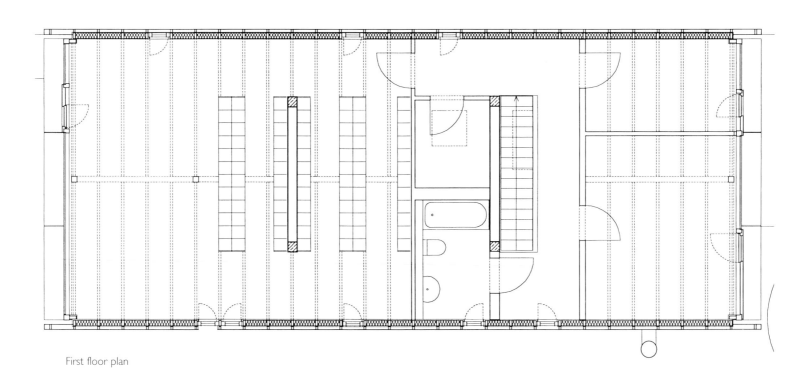

First floor plan

The ground floor was built in-situ, while the first floor was made from prefabricated pieces lifted into place using a light wooden structure. This combination speeded up the construction process.

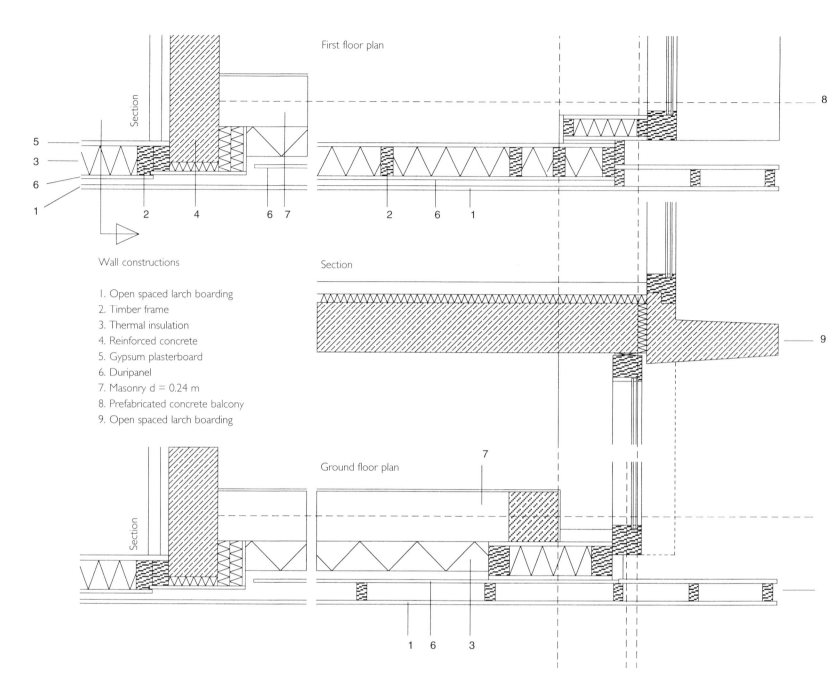

First floor plan

Section

Wall constructions

1. Open spaced larch boarding
2. Timber frame
3. Thermal insulation
4. Reinforced concrete
5. Gypsum plasterboard
6. Duripanel
7. Masonry d = 0.24 m
8. Prefabricated concrete balcony
9. Open spaced larch boarding

Ground floor plan

Elevation

Bearth & Deplazes
The Hinsbrunner House

Scharans, Switzerland

On the edge of the compact town-center of Scharans, this building nestles on sparsely populated land, dotted with individual dwellings and with loosely defined property limits. There is no sensation of a hierarchy of public and private land and property. In order to highlight its situation, the building cuts out a horizontal plane framed by the house and the garage building, forming a terrace on the slope.

This terrace cannot be accessed readily from the outside. It is covered with a fine layer of sand, with no plants. A path of uneven slabs leads to the house. Footsteps leave marks on the sand, making the view from the gallery or sunroom of the house more inviting. The neighboring house blocks a direct view of the valley, but as the building is orientated so that its long, blind facade is near the back of the house, a view of the surroundings is nevertheless opened up: southwards, onto the Beverin mountains, and northwards towards the mouth of the Domleschg valley. This orientation gives a foretaste of the logic governing the interior structure of the space which contains the stairway, the kitchen units and the bathroom: freely distributed, with sub-divisions to these spaces.

The walls are further reinforced by the gallery framework, and its system of leaning pillars. This made it possible to glaze the front façades fully, with no further static constructions.

Wooden box beams were used for the roof. All of the wall and roof elements in this building were prefabricated and mounted on site by means of the standard element assembly system.

Photographs: Ralph Feiner

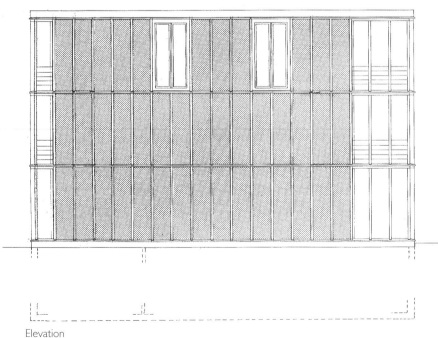

Elevation

188

The north and south façades are fully glazed. The gallery framework is perpendiculer to the load-bearing walls, which are strengthened by a structure of leaning pillars.

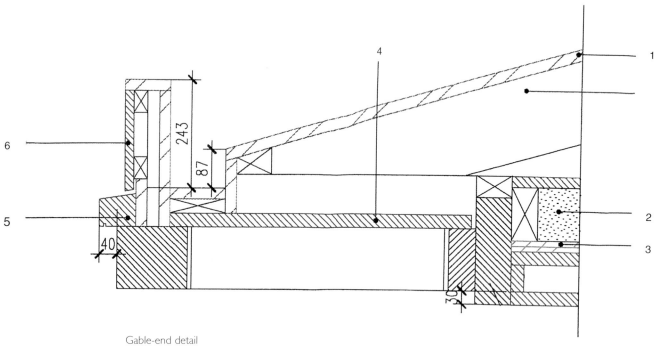

Gable-end detail
1. Lintel 100/180 mm
2. Cellulose insulation 55 kg/m
3. Plywood C/C 12.5 mm
4. Larch boards 62 mm
5. Larch seat 45/80 mm
6. Larch formwork N+K 20 mm

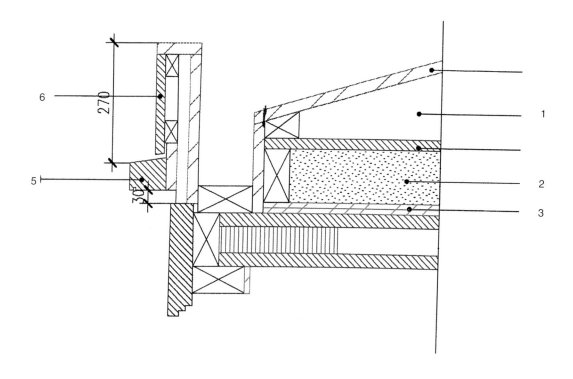

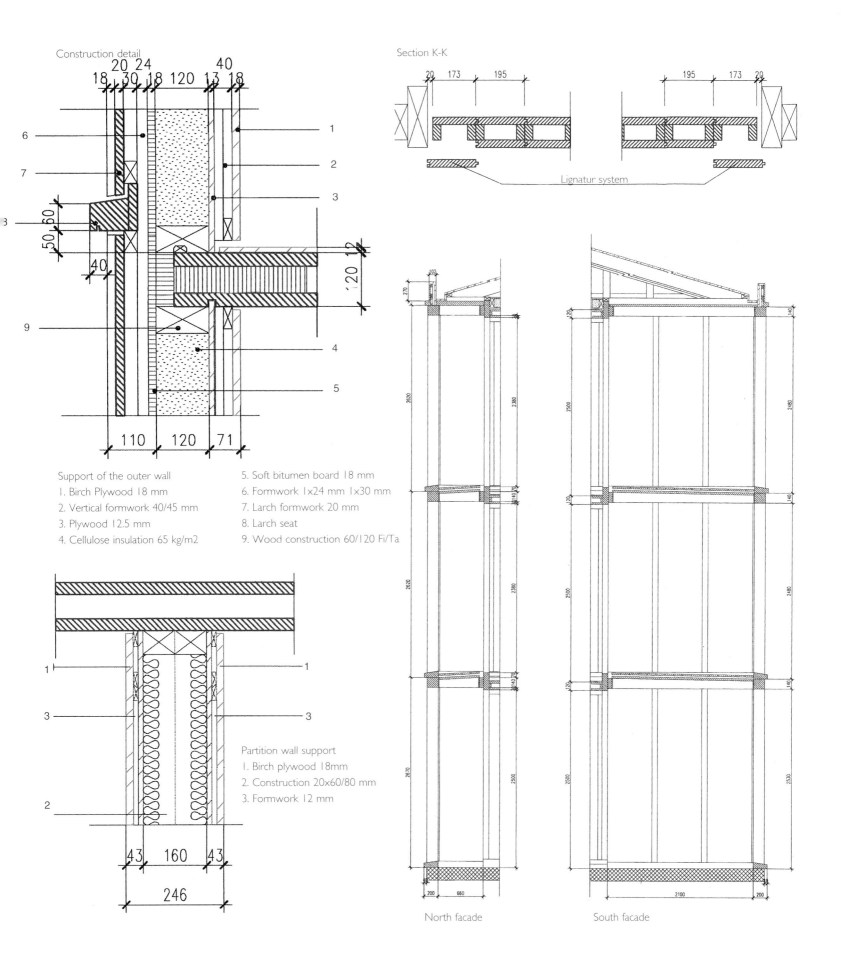

Construction detail

Section K-K

Lignatur system

Support of the outer wall
1. Birch Plywood 18 mm
2. Vertical formwork 40/45 mm
3. Plywood 12.5 mm
4. Cellulose insulation 65 kg/m2

5. Soft bitumen board 18 mm
6. Formwork 1x24 mm 1x30 mm
7. Larch formwork 20 mm
8. Larch seat
9. Wood construction 60/120 Fi/Ta

Partition wall support
1. Birch plywood 18mm
2. Construction 20x60/80 mm
3. Formwork 12 mm

North facade

South facade

193

Marco Savorelli
Nicola's Home

Milan, Italy

On the concept evolution of the recuperation possibilities of an old roof attic is founded the bet between the client and designers: to start from zero, working in abstract on "home system" functions and utilities, beginning from recuperation of a unified, primary, elementary space, translating old function into new, mitigated and simplified forms.

Discrete presence, operative spaces like bathroom, kitchen and wardrobe translate themselves into monolithic volumes that, reduced into simple forms, gain plastic authority, creating new routes, background, bonds and articulations of the perceptive space system.

This is a project where the historical memory of the site meets a rigorous formal research. A well balanced experimentation with new spaces preserving the existing quality of light. The result is a playful alternation of volumes and moods, a fluid exchange between the existing and the designed space. These are characteristics of a project which evolved from the intense dialogue between the architect and the client, aiming to achieve a minimalist aesthetics and at the same time volumetric and functional complexity. This is not a mere operation of interior decoration but the creation of volumes to be lived in and "live with" in a completely modern and innovative way. The space acquires both a jocose and a reflexive quality.

When entering this apartment the visual impact is instantaneous —a nearly flash-like perception of the space— which reveals the equilibrium between matter and light. The natural daylight traces delicate designs on the neat surfaces, shadows in perpetual movement creating a simple and primordial game of light and darkness.

Photographs: Matteo Piazza

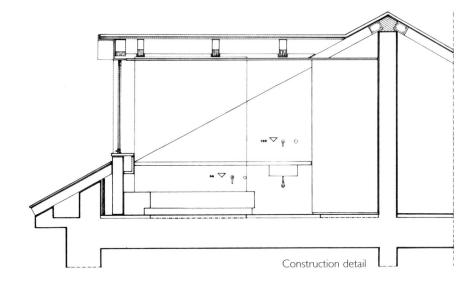

Construction detail

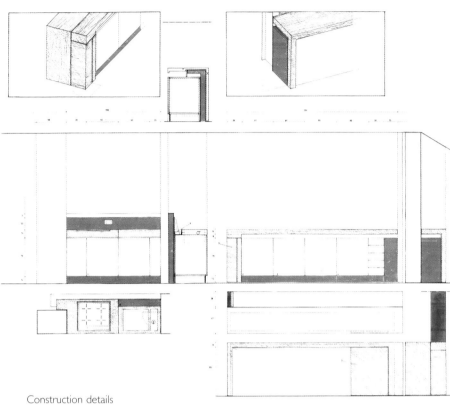

Construction details

Floor plan

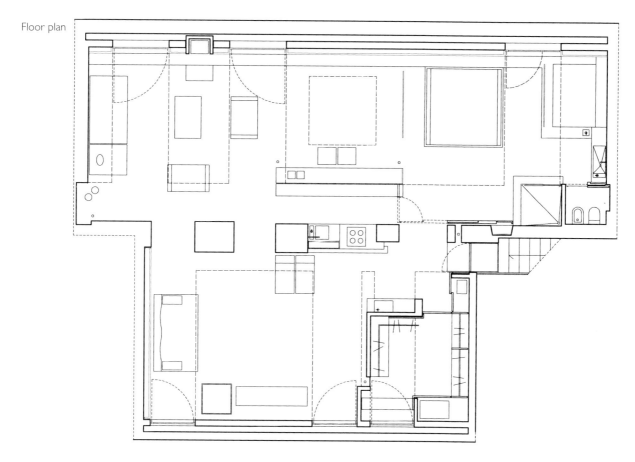

The distribution of spaces follows an open plan, with minimum partitions and a constant search for fluency and dialogue between the different environments. The use of a limited range of materials contributes to this objective.

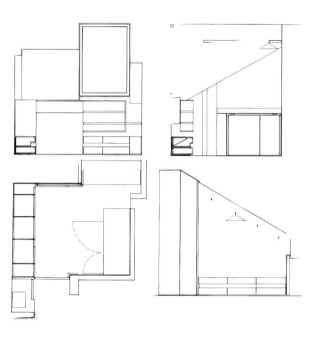

Construction details

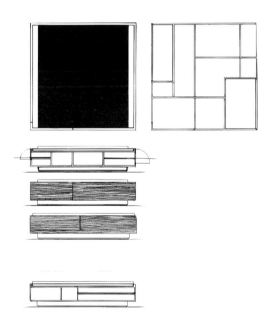

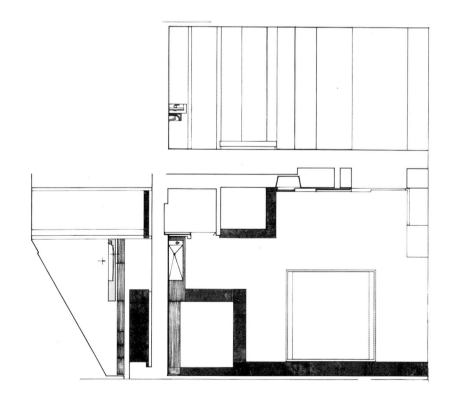

Tadao Ando
Lee House

Tokyo, Japan

This private house is situated on a hill in the suburbs of Funabashi not far from the Tokyo metropolitan center and occupies a site area of 5210 ft². The location of the site at an intersection and its comfortable size (in comparison with more normal dimensions in Japanese houses) have allowed the creation of numerous additional spaces to the house: courtyards, gardens and terraces.

Small garden courtyards of varying character are stacked on different levels within the house in order to grant each one a distinct realm and infuse the house with greater variety.

Overall, the house has a three-level rectangular core with a 16'4" x 68'9" floor plan. An internal atrium is positioned in the mid-section of this rectangular structure, with rooms positioned at either end. The rooms face each other across the atrium at staggered half-floor intervals, and are connected by ramps running parallel to the court.

The ground floor houses the living room and dining room where the family gathers, while individual bedrooms are arranged on the upper floors. The gentle, green slope of the garden draws close where it is viewed from the dining room. This garden invites nature into the lives of the residents, while maintaining the house's privacy by obstructing visibility from the exterior. The different garden courtyards ensure a dwelling space that offers its occupants continual rediscovery, within daily life, of their relationship with the city and nature.

Photographs: Mitsuo Matsuoka

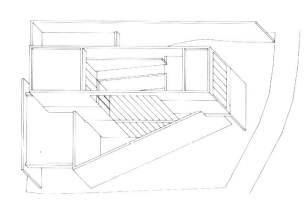

A dramatic contrast is struck between high concrete walls, the intensity of the light provided by large openings and the subtle yet notable presence of nature.

Tadao Ando skilfully combines the complexity of the spaces with the simplicity of the house's rectangular base.

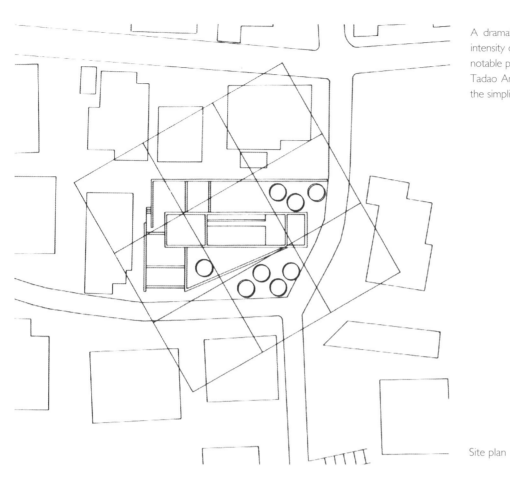

Site plan

The bedrooms, at staggered half-floor intervals, are connected by a ramp running parallel to the courtyard.

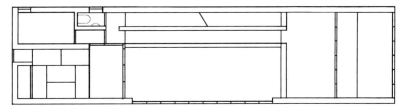

Stepped levels, courtyards and terraces add complexity to the project, which is nevertheless regulated by a coherent system.

First floor plan

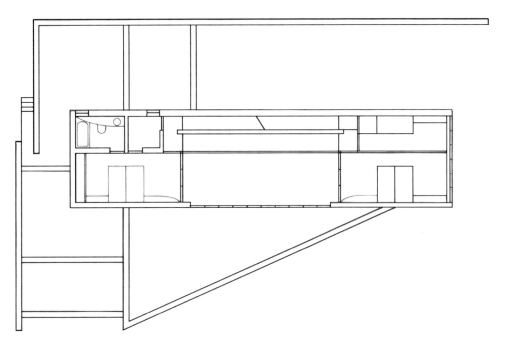

Ground floor plan

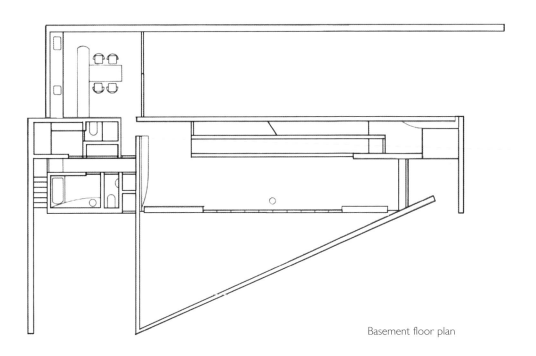

Basement floor plan

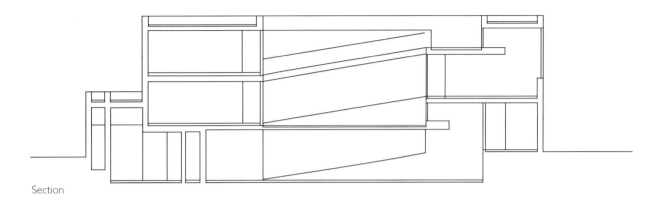

Section

Patkau Architects
Barnes House

Nanaimo, Canada

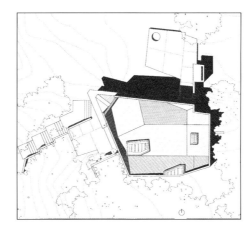

Site plan

Set in wild landscape on the edge of Vancouver Island, this house has a tectonic clarity and material expressiveness informed by place and culture. The project is a modern rein- terpretation of the pragmatically romantic building traditions of Canada's West Coast, an exploration of the relationship between landscape and architecture. Poised on the edge of a rocky outcrop overlooking the Georgia Strait, the house appears as an isolated object set against the landscape. Douglas firs and mossy rocks form a craggy backdrop to the crisply articulated geometries. The house is partially embedded in a depression, exploiting the topography while also offering a series of framed views of the landscape. A path rises towards the west elevation, which tapers to a sharp prow marked by an overhanging roof of thin steel plate. Wall planes extend beyond the building line, sheltering a small terrace and channel- ing visitors to the main entrance on the lower level.

Screened from the entrance by a freestanding storage panel, a studio. To the rear, a small guest suite. Running along the north edge of the house, the stairs lead up to the main piano nobile living and dining space. The master bedroom is on the south side, with a kitchen tucked in directly above the guest suite. Space is fluid and informal, divided and defined by screens and storage units. A larger outdoor space with views over the Georgia Strait connects with the north elevation through a tall glazed wall that opens up the opaque flanks of the house.

The main building elements - stucco walls, a steel canopy, timber roof and concrete floor - are compositionally and materially dis- tinct, giving a lucid, tectonic expressiveness. Arboreal columns and an undulating ceiling evoke the surrounding forest. Rippling over the corrugated joists of the roof structure, light is filtered through skylights, dappling the interior in a gentle luminance.

The narrow glazed face, beetle-browed roof canopy and high parapet walls allude to the great anthropomorphic totem poles of indigenous Pacific Coast tribes. The grey of the stucco ren- der blends with the bark of the Douglas firs and the slim tim- ber frames of the doors and windows are stained a rich rust to mimic the trunks of arbutus trees on the site. Conceived as an instrument for experiencing the landscape, this house is a good example of elegance, simplicity and aptness.

Photographs: James Dow

Ground floor plan

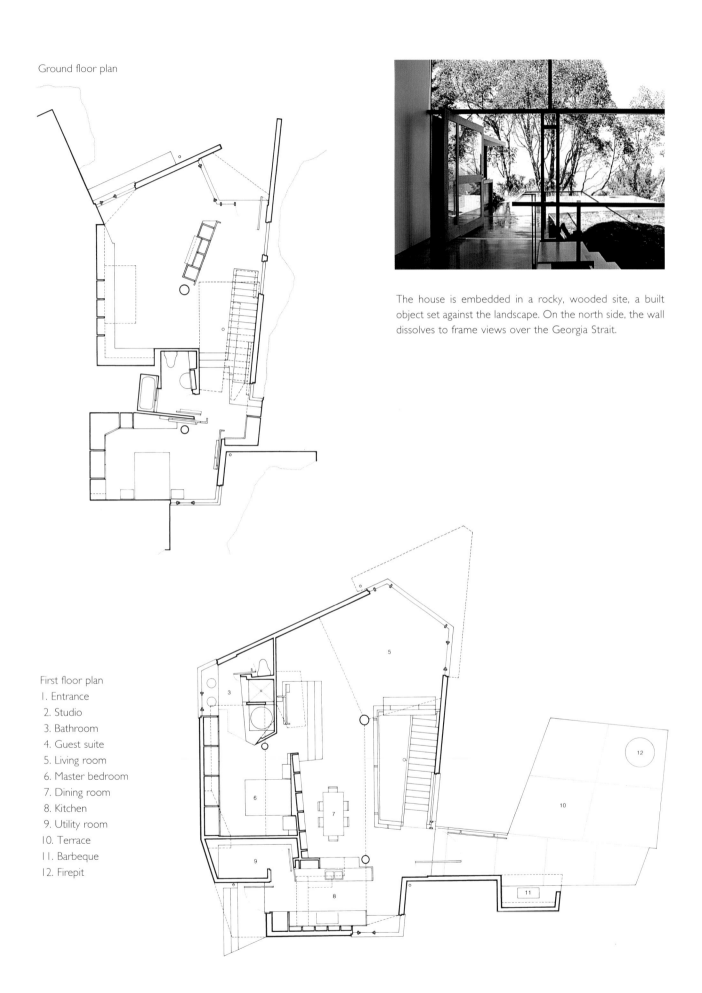

The house is embedded in a rocky, wooded site, a built object set against the landscape. On the north side, the wall dissolves to frame views over the Georgia Strait.

First floor plan
1. Entrance
2. Studio
3. Bathroom
4. Guest suite
5. Living room
6. Master bedroom
7. Dining room
8. Kitchen
9. Utility room
10. Terrace
11. Barbeque
12. Firepit

Screens and storage units divide the fluid, informal spaces. The master bedroom is concealed behind a shelving unit in the living area.

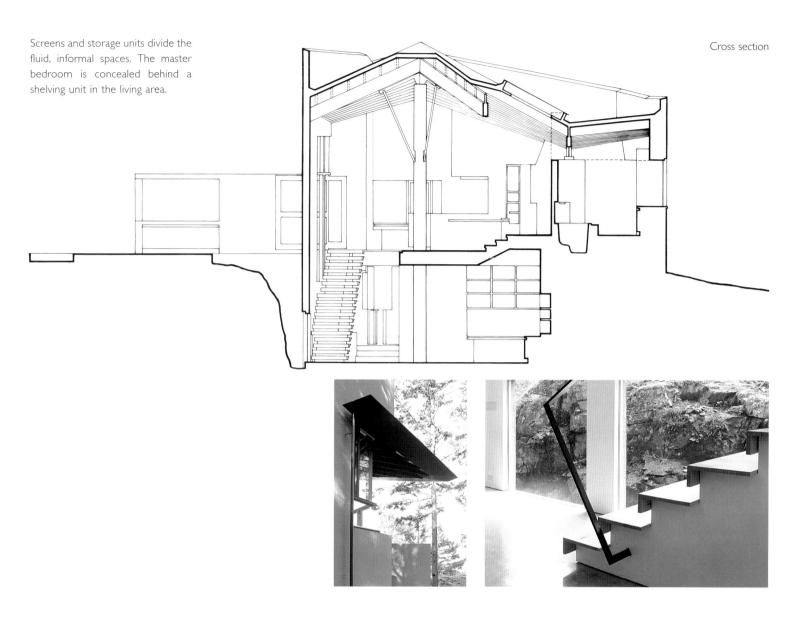

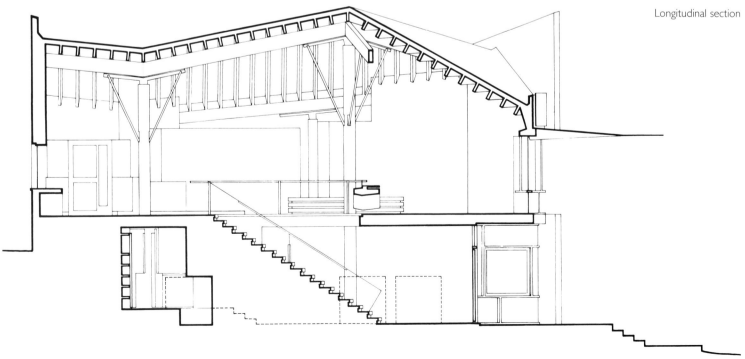

Longitudinal section

Patrick Hernandez
Pavillon de Garde

Arsac, France

The residence for the custodian of Arsac Castle, in the heart of the Médoc, is located in the castle's entrance driveway. It is a more radical proposal than that usually seen in individual dwellings, as it is sealed off to its immediate surroundings, yet open to the sky.

Parked delivery cars can be seen in front of the castle's gate to the north, and a major road lies to the east, while to the south and west; the gaze slides unobstructed over a sprawling expanse of grass. The lack of scenic value in this desert-like environment gave the architect the idea of constructing a veritable oasis, a self-sufficient unit, which would fold in on itself, able to find its own identity. Blind walls, an affirmation of introversion, are this structure's response to the immensity of these surroundings. The vertical views through the roof respond to the vast horizons. In fact, this oasis precisely defines its own boundaries on the surrounding land: the wall, made from Douglas pine, is extended to the gate, defining the border of the vineyard on one side and, on the other, the private exterior space. A small patio with a sliding door lets additional light into the dwelling from the side. The entire residence -kitchen, sitting room, dining room and bedrooms- benefits from the natural light provided by the glass ceiling. This steel-framed glass structure is part of the attempt to adapt the living space to the industrialized systems used in the construction of greenhouses, a method which this architect had previously used in a restaurant near Bordeaux.

In this type of construction, which gives precedence to vertical views, the garden does not encircle the dwelling, but rather is placed on top of it. The metal wall support structure is extended beyond the roof and forms a pergola designed to hold plants and flowers.

Photographs: Vincent Monthiers

215

Site plan

Ground floor plan

Roof plan

The custodian's residence at Arsac Castle is isolated in a location of such mediocre qualities that the architect made the radical decision to eliminate all lateral views and to reinforce its opening to the sky above with a glass roof.

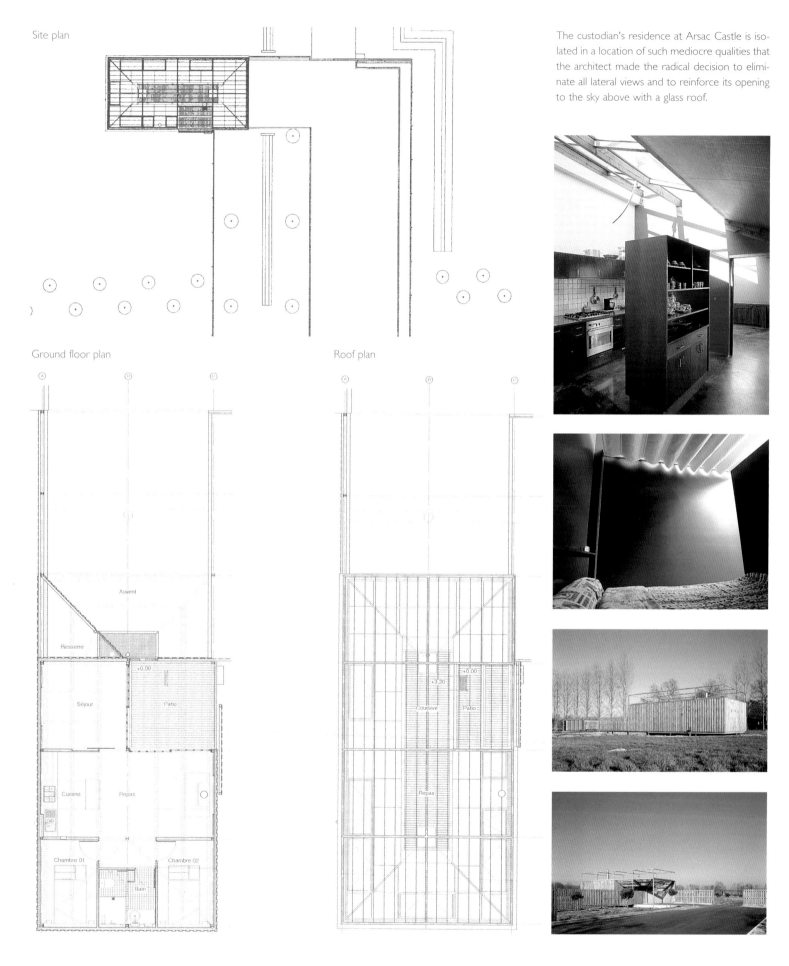

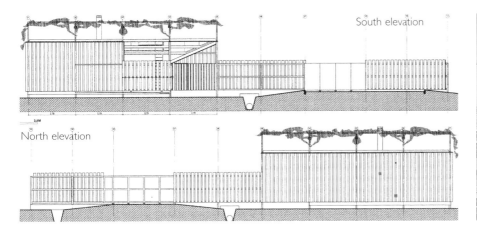

South elevation

North elevation

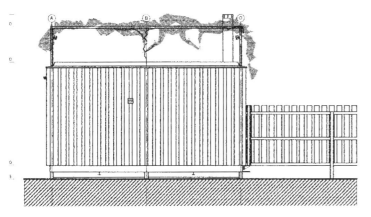

West elevation

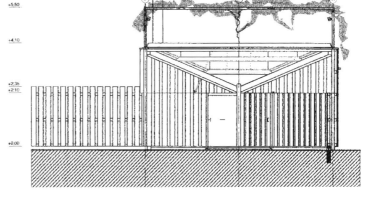

East elevation

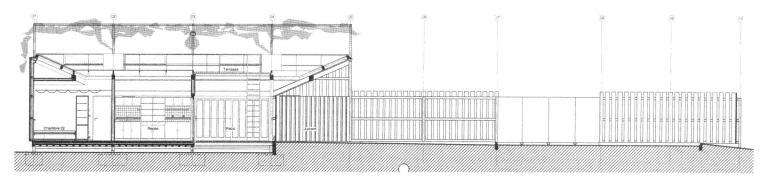

Section A-A'

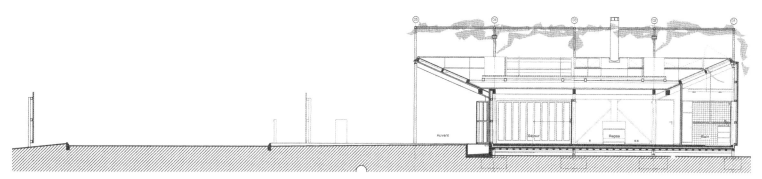

Section B-B'

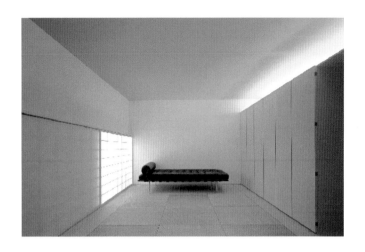

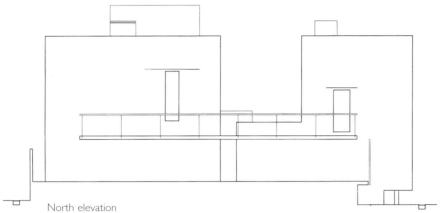

North elevation

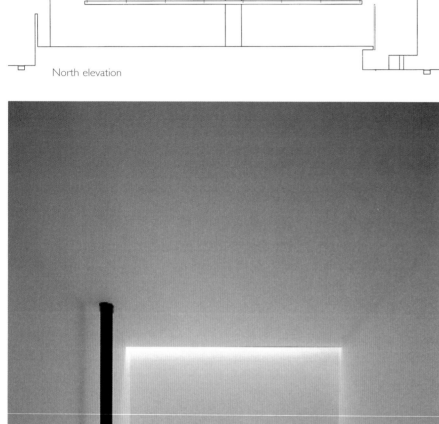

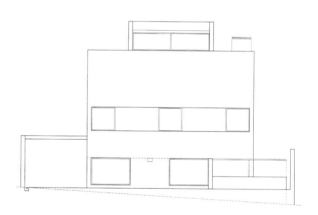

East elevation (east building)

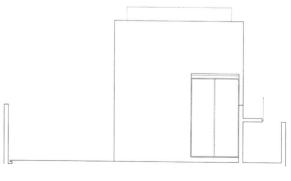

East elevation (west building)

John Pawson
Faggionato Apartment

London, UK

The apartment was to be created in part of a 1960s complex of laboratories built by the Gas Board in the heart of a south west suburb of London overlooking the river Thames. A developer had acquired the building when the Gas Board moved out and converted it into a series of shells for individual apartments. The clients had bought two of these units, which combined to form a vast L-shaped space of 600 m^2 - the size of two or three conventional London terraced houses.

Here the clients were an art dealer and her financier husband. They had known the architect for some time. They realized that they were undertaking a whole new way of life —their previous home had been a very traditional apartment. The move required a new approach to domestic habits, new ways of dealing with possessions, indeed new possessions —the old furniture was not going to fit into so different an interior— and new ways for the couple of relating to each other and their children.

The architect wanted to create the sense of endless, unencumbered space. There was enough height to create a mezzanine level —in fact two mezzanine decks, one for parents, another for children and housekeeper— but also the scope to leave extensive areas of double-height space. As a result a sequence of spaces which incorporated both private and more open arrangements were provided.

The oak floors, laid in random widths, add rhythm and warmth to the interior spaces. The dining room and kitchen are accommodated under the mezzanine and screened from the main living area by a smoked glass wall. The three children´s bedrooms share a mezzanine deck. Two deep, stepped shelves form workspace overlooking the double height slice of space in front of the windows.

Photographs: Richard Glover

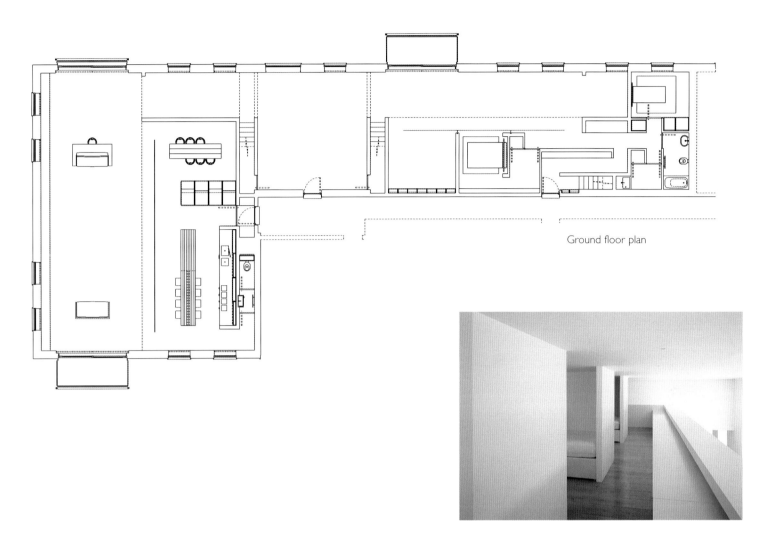

Ground floor plan

First floor plan

Hermann & Valentiny et Associès
Haus am Seitweg

Klosterneuburg, Vienna, Austria

The house is situated on a relatively steep incline in the midst of a development of single-family houses, setting a significant alternative to the rapidly expanding gabled roof surroundings. For the house does contain a play on the otherwise standard gabled form, the sixty degree slope to the concrete slab of the roof looks like a metaphor, albeit a contemporary one. The lamella skin on the west facade, which casts a comfortable shadow onto a deck-like terrace, especially in the afternoon, also adds to the marked appearance of the building.

The interior concept is very simple. From the street, one enters the accommodation on a level with a very open living room and the kitchen. From here a steep staircase leads to the client's workspace and to a spare bedroom. Below, with direct access to the garden, are the bedrooms for the children and their parents. The rigorous limitation of materials in the house makes a pleasant impression, naked concrete with thoroughly "painterly" flaws, wood, glass, concrete and, in the bathroom, Eternit. The views within the house are also pleasant, from the reception level down to the children, for example. And the orientation outwards: the wide panorama offered to the occupants in autumn when the foliage thins is particularly spectacular.

Photographs: G.G. Kirchner

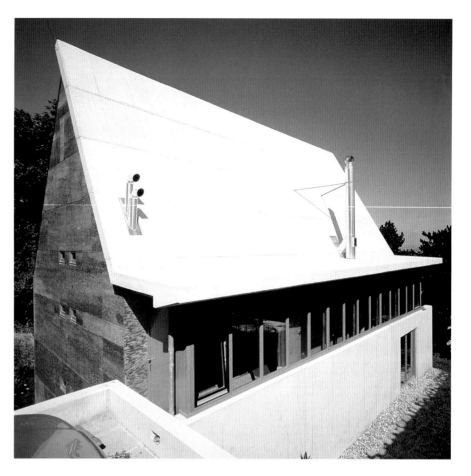

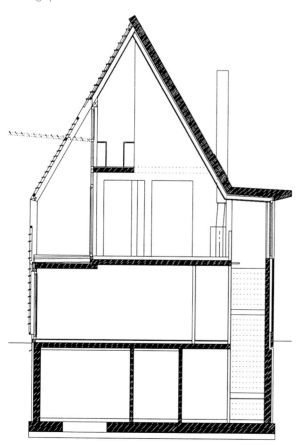

Section AA

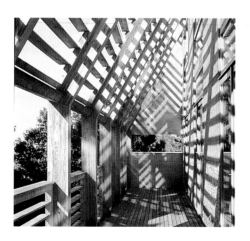

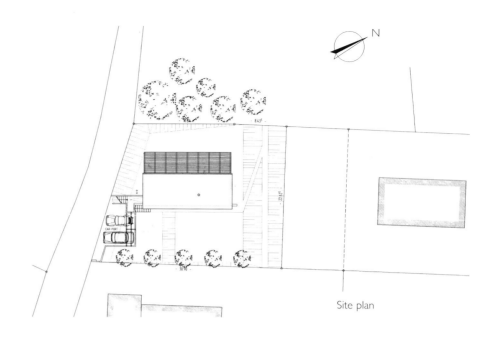

Site plan

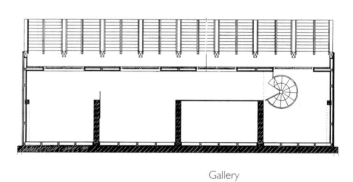

Gallery

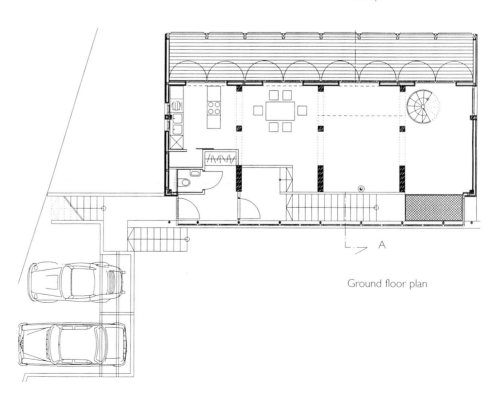

Ground floor plan

Limestone was used for the exterior cladding. The contrast between this and the white of the roof endows this structure with a dynamic, innovative character.

First floor plan

A

233

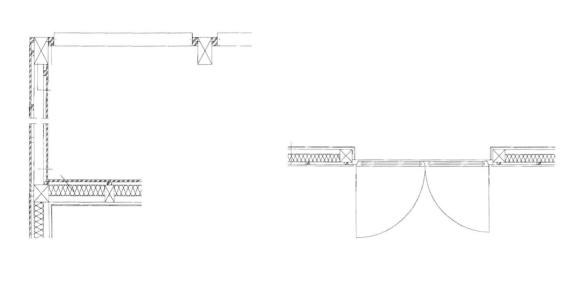
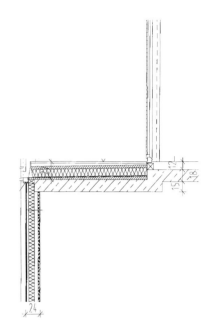

Section details

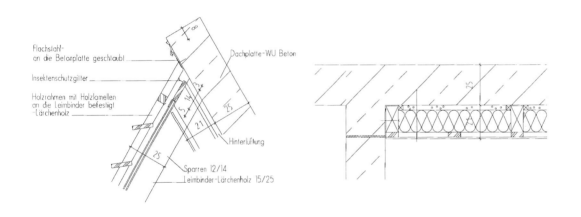

Flachstahl-
an die Betonplatte geschraubt

Insektenschutzgitter

Holzrahmen mit Holzlamellen
an die Leimbinder befestigt
-Lärchenholz

Dachplatte-WU Beton

Hinterlüftung

Sparren 12/14
Leimbinder-Lärchenholz 15/25

The glazing of one of the gables of the double-sloping roof has allowed the architects to infuse the home's interior with natural light and views.

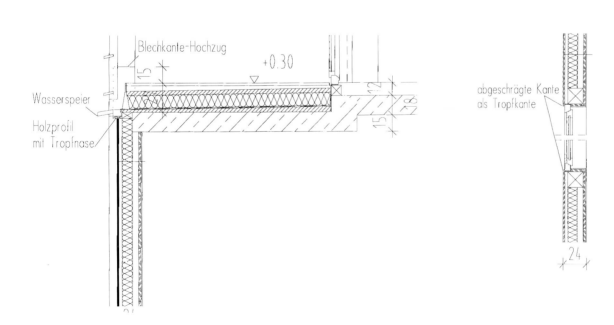

Blechkante-Hochzug

+0.30

Wasserspeier

Holzprofil
mit Tropfnase

abgeschrägte Kante
als Tropfkante

Araceli Manzano & Esther Flavià
House in Argentona

Argentona, Spain

This dwelling, located on a particularly long rectangular plot (5x22 m), maintains the structure of the houses that are typical in the area: ground floor with direct access from the street, first floor and a small court at the rear. The intervention aimed to respect the existing structure as far as possible, but due to its extremely deteriorated state it was only possible to conserve the stone party walls, the front facade and the wooden structure.

The roofing bricks and a wooden beam structure had been concealed behind a vaulted drop ceiling, which had to be demolished. The wooden structure of the roof was repaired and the tiles were replaced, over a layer of insulation. Removing the drop ceiling increased the height of the first floor, making it possible to build a mezzanine, formed by a light metal structure covered with wooden boards.

The original front facade was conserved, although the woodwork had to be replaced, and wooden shutters were added. The rear facade was modified to increase the size of the openings and obtain better lighting. A sizeable landscaped courtyard was created by the demolition of the small buildings adjacent to the house.

On the ground floor the kitchen was located on the facade, so it became a particularly attractive element due to its situation on the street and the amount of daylight that it receives. The rest of the floor is a large living/dining room that opens onto the court through a large wooden window. A system of sliding doors was used between the living room, the kitchen and the access, thus creating an extremely fluid relation between the rooms.

On the first floor, two double rooms with dressing room and bathroom, situated symmetrically in relation to the floor plan, use the front and rear facades to ventilate directly to the street. The totally open floor plan of the mezzanine was created for use as an office or gym, but could easily be converted into two independent rooms.

The location of the rooms on the facade leaves free the central space, where double-height spaces not coinciding in the whole height are used to develop the stairs. The treatment of the double spaces tempers the view of the real height of the house from all the floors.

Photographs: Eugeni Pons

236

237

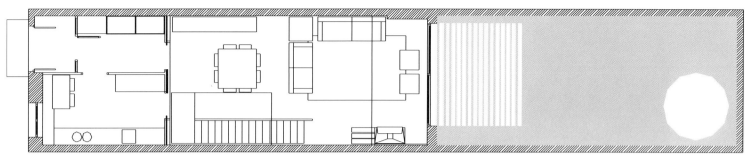

Ground floor plan

First floor plan

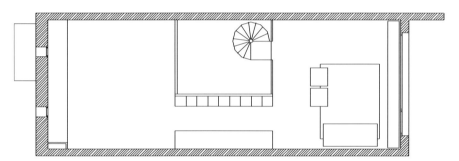

Roof floor plan

The floor cladding is of waxed chestnut floorboards; the long side wall of the living room was painted with iron oxide, and all the wooden elements (wardrobes, banisters, door frames) with colored enamel in order to highlight the volumetrics.

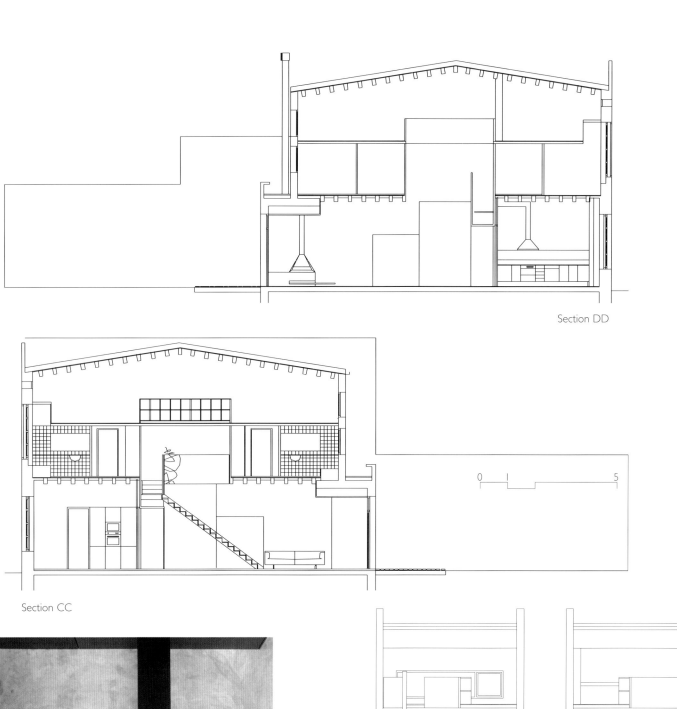

Section DD

Section CC

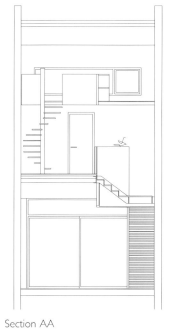

Section AA

Section BB

On the first floor, two double rooms with dressing room and bathroom, situated symmetrically in relation to the floor plan, use the front and rear facades for ventilation.

FOBA
Aura House

Tokyo, Japan

In the amorphous complexity of central Tokyo, urban structure occurs at scales imperceptible to the pedestrian observer. Forms are either incoherent or irrelevant; the urban experience is a succession of interior spaces.

Here, a house requires few facilities. To eat, you go to a restaurant; to bathe, you go to the sento (public baths); to exercise, you go to the gym; to be entertained, you go to the cinema. The ultimate Tokyo house is somehow like an art gallery: an empty, inward-looking space, perhaps with unusual lighting.

The Aura house is located in a typical Japanese "eel's nest" site: an alley 3.5 meters wide by 21.5 meters long. The challenge was to bring light and air into the center of the house. Rather than using the traditional tsubo-niwa (courtyard garden), the architects opted instead for optimizing both the available light and the potential floor area.

Concrete walls were run down either side of the site and a translucent membrane was stretched between them. In order to sustain tension in the roof fabric, a complex curve was created by making the two walls identical but reversed. Cylindrical concrete beams brace the two walls. The opposing ridge lines cause the orientation of the beams to twist along the length of the building - despite appearances, a rational structural solution. The fabric skin filters sunlight by day, and glows by night: the building pulses, "breathing" light with the 24-hour rhythm of the city.

Photographs: Tohru Waki / Shokokusha

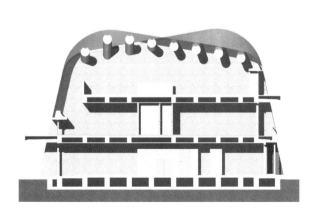

Site plan

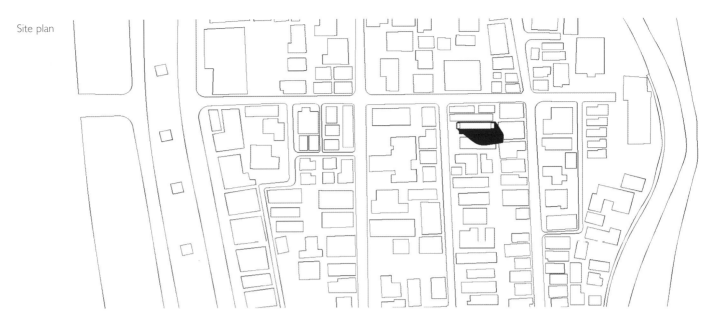

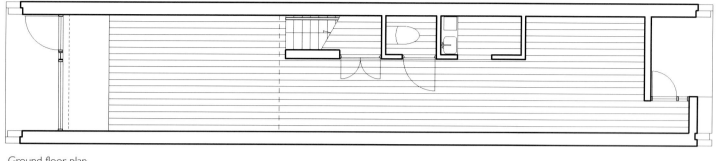

Ground floor plan

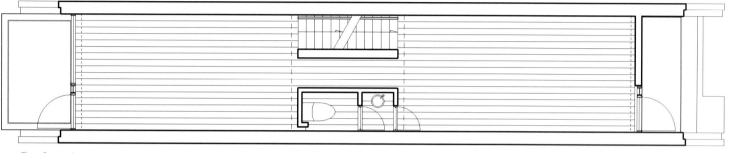

First floor plan

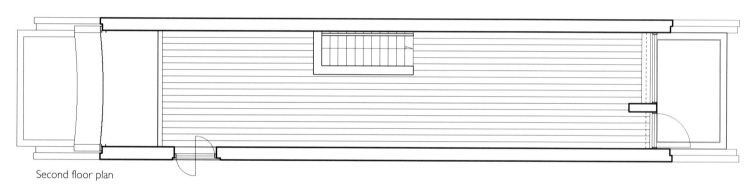

Second floor plan

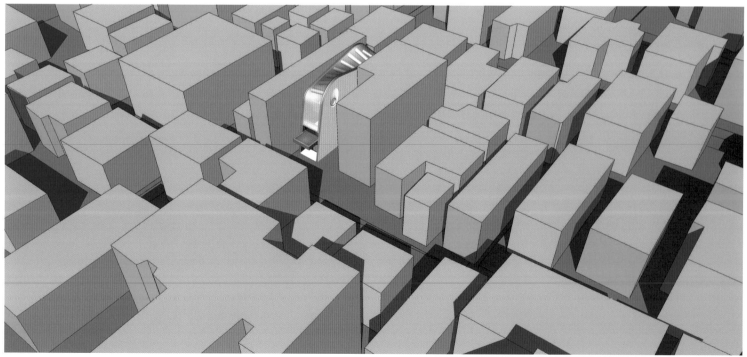

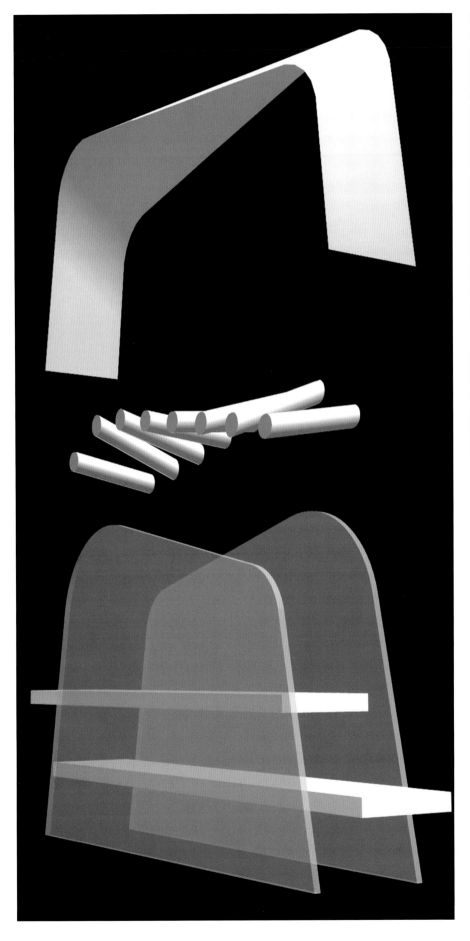

Longitudinal section

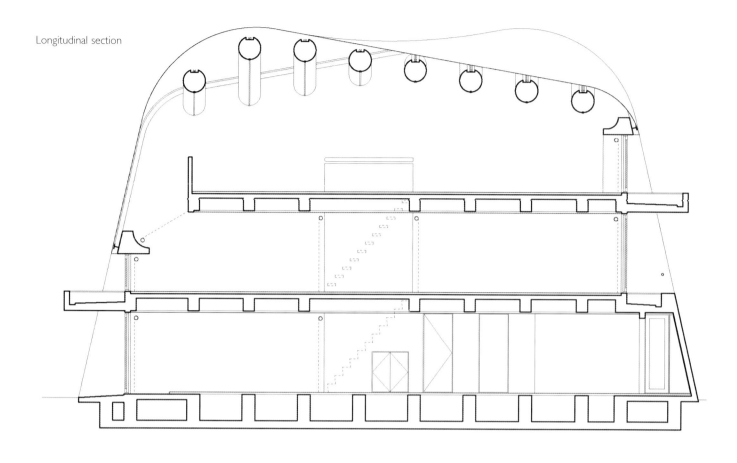

Side elevation

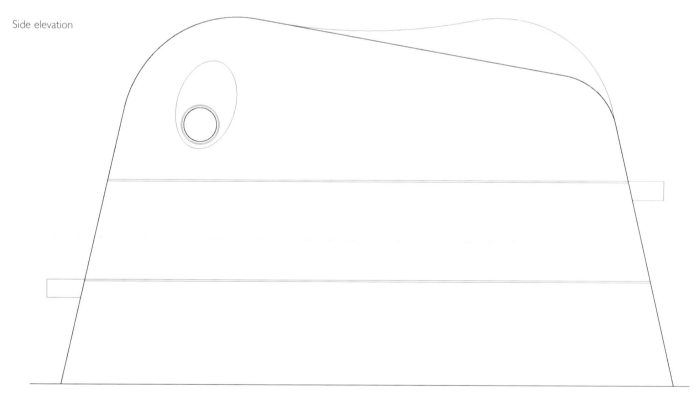

248

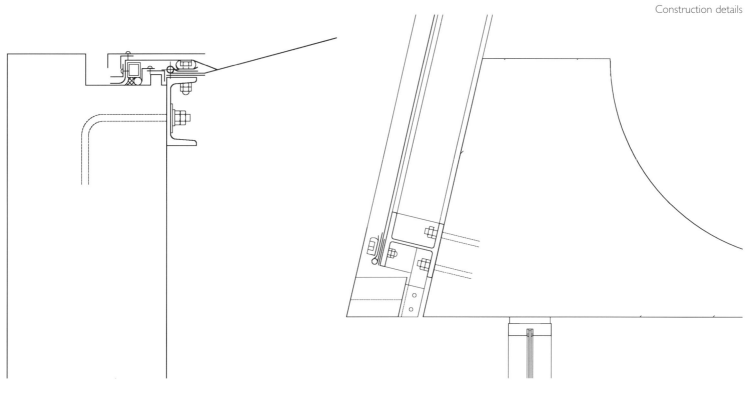

José Cruz Ovalle
House in Santo Domingo

Rocas de Santo Domingo, Chile

This dwelling located on a slope facing the sea is raised above the land on reinforced concrete slabs and built entirely in wood, thus providing an effective and aesthetic solution to the problem of damp that is often found in coastal areas.

In this building of 350 m^2 on a plot of 1135 m^2 the architects attempted to configure a space "illuminated" by the surrounding landscape and not simply dominated by it, as often happens in houses located on the seafront. The seascape usually steals the interior space by dissipating it toward the horizon in a single direction. To respond to this presence, the architects invented the "counter-view", which seeks its power in the maximum expansion of a space that opens its depth in multiple directions. This is achieved by rotating the house around a courtyard that is open to the sea and sheltered from the prevailing winds, in order to form a double interior. This rotation partly accommodates the slope of the land by means of the different horizontal levels of the floor, as a way of multiplying the vertical lines in order to create the oblique depths that measure and graduate the characteristic "up" and "down" relationship of a sloping site.

The "counterview" is thus here the abstraction that proposes an oriented but not directed interior and that balances the eloquence of the landscape by means of a space developed in different directions that relates proximity and distance. This exercise allows the surrounding dual elements (the land and its slope, the neighboring houses and their gardens, the extension of the beach and the reef, the distance of the sea and the horizon) to illuminate the interior of this house without dominating it.

Photographs: Juan Purcell

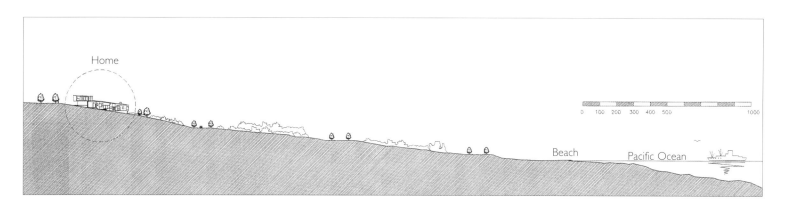

Home

0 100 200 300 400 500   1000

Beach

Pacific Ocean

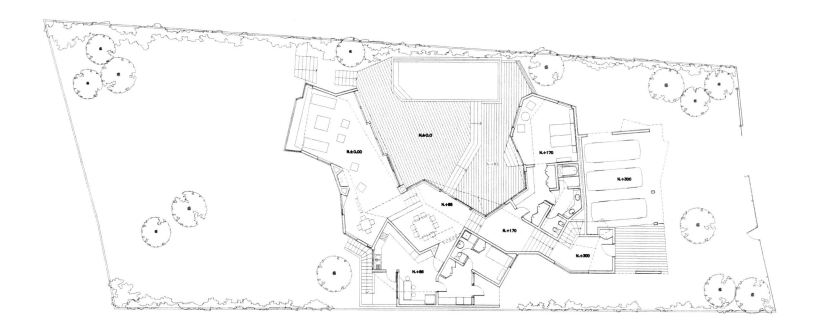

Ground floor plan

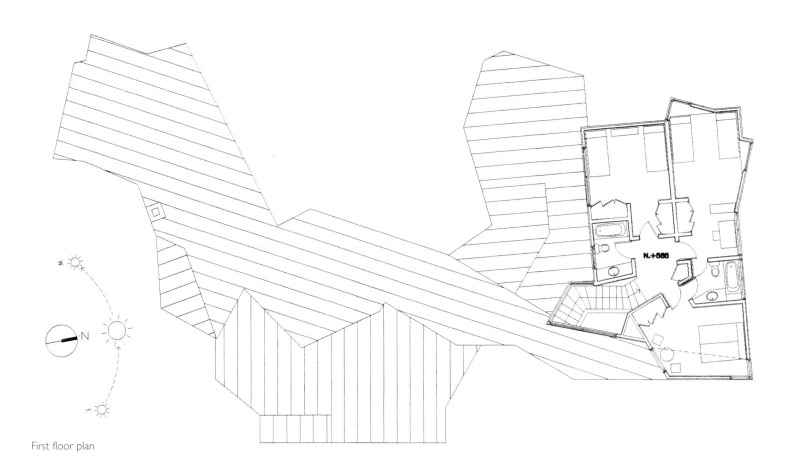

First floor plan

The change of orientation of the wooden lattice that lines the interior of this dwelling creates a visual spectacle in which the different axes, cuts and openings play a major role.

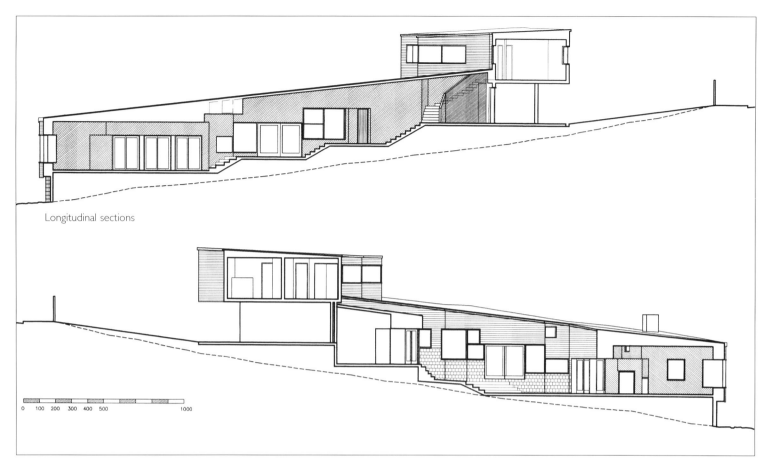

Longitudinal sections

0 100 200 300 400 500   1000

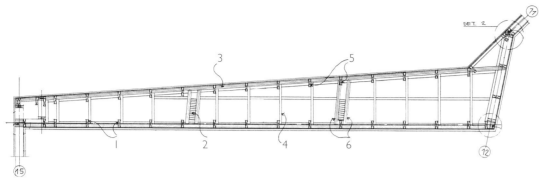

Horizontal section, details of windows
1. Stud 2"x6"
2. Wooden pillar 110x400
3. Wooden beam 42x180
4. 2"x6" pieces of drop ceiling structure
5. Studs 2"x6" with cavity at bottom to nail them to beam 42x180
6. Wooden assembly 42x180

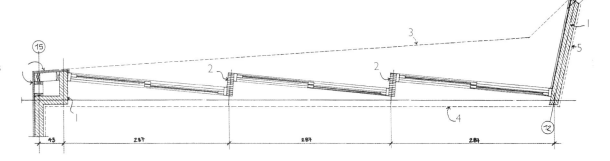

Construction detail of windows
1. Reinforced concrete wall
2. Wooden pillar 110x400
3. Projection of drop ceiling
4. Projection of drop ceiling
5. Projection of exterior siding

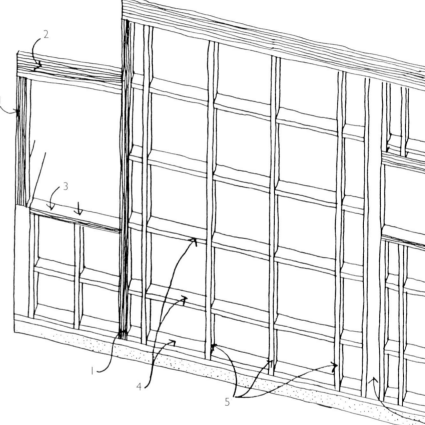

Isometric projection of the structure of the main facade, 2nd floor
1. Wooden stud
2. Wooden beam 42x150 covered edge
3. Wooden windowsill 42x95
4. Chain 2"x4"
5. Stud 2"x4"
6. Upper sill 2"x4"
7. Wooden lintel 95x110
8. Continuous sill 2"x4"
9. 2nd floor slab
10. Stud 2"x4"
11. Wooden beam 42x150 lintel
12. Wooden beam 42x150 windowsill
13. Cladding sheet 2"x6"

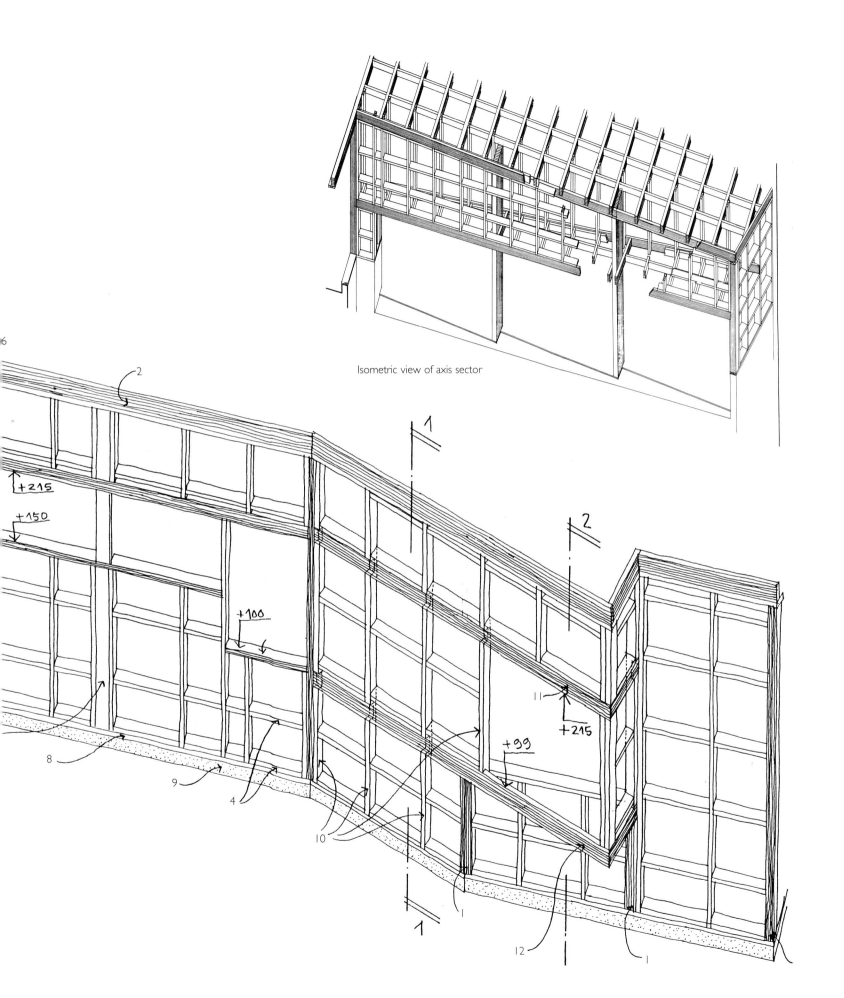

Isometric view of axis sector

+215

+150

+100

+215

+99

2

1

1

2

11

8

9

4

10

12

259

Thom Maine-Morphosis
Blades Residence

Santa Barbara, USA

In June 1990 several hundred homes in the coastal hills of Santa Barbara were destroyed by fire. The clients decided to reframe this catastrophic experience as a catalyst to reinvent their day-to-day existence. Unlike their neighbors who took more "conventional" approaches, they decided to build a house "like nothing they had ever seen before".

The fire left a charred landscape with a gentle sloping grade, several boulders and a cluster of native oaks. Given its suburban/rural context, the introspective strategy for an enclosed project was explored.

Due to the very modest budget, design and craftsmanship were given priority over expensive materials from the very first moment. The 3800 feet of interior ground area is organized as three main spaces adjacent to five smaller exterior rooms, each one a linear sequence of overlapping zones in which the boundaries of public and private spaces are intentionally blurred. Interior light is modulated through subtle openings and recesses that create a sculpted space. The couple shares a very open bedroom, yet each has their individual studios at opposite ends of the house.

The upper story studio has expansive views from a corner window that has been carved out as well as an exterior catwalk. The ground floor studio/gallery is a separate wing with clerestory windows and no exterior views.

Photographs: Kim Zwarts

260

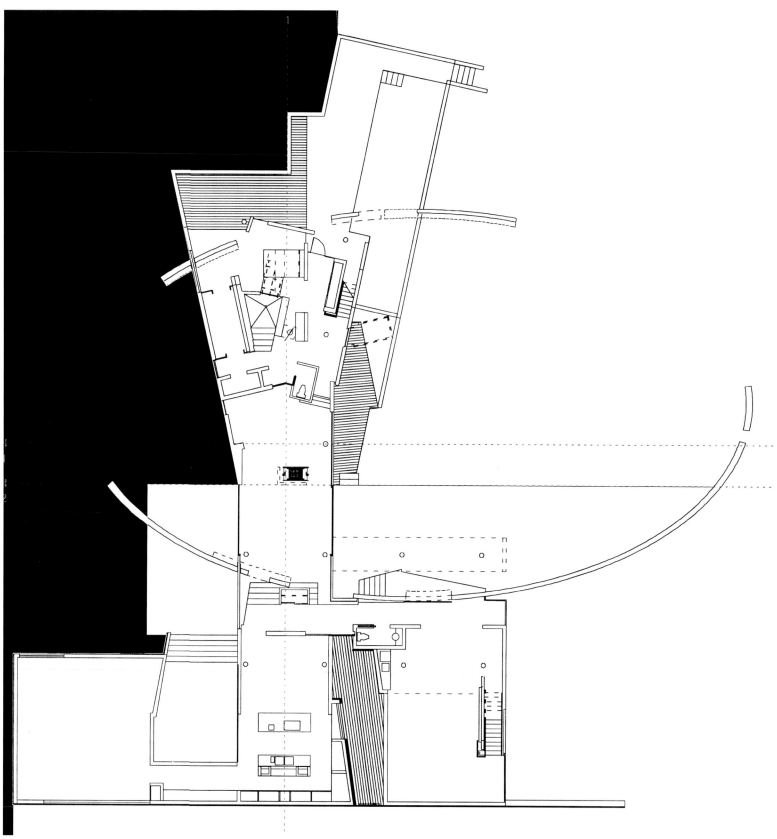

Ground floor plan

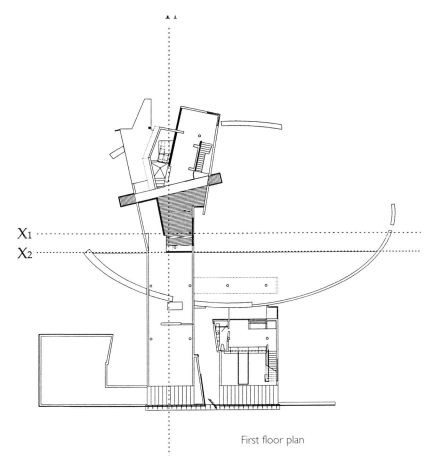

X₁ ......
X₂ ......

First floor plan

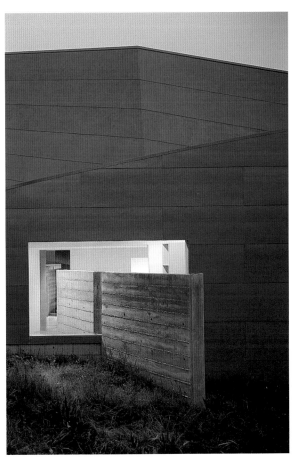

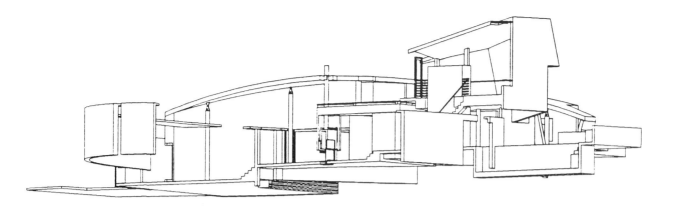

Cross-sections

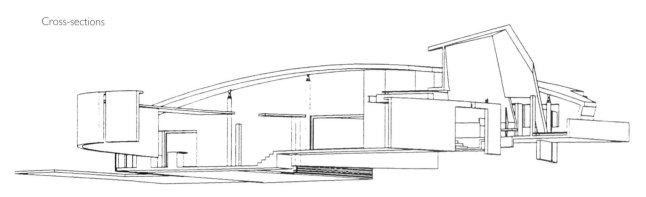

The interior of the dwelling is organized as a large single space that is almost entirely uninterrupted.

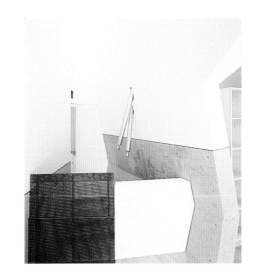

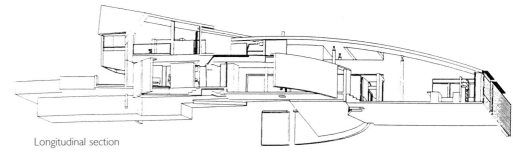

Longitudinal section

Torsten Neeland
House of Dr. Shank

Hamburg, Germany

The building, which dates from the beginning of the century, contains an apartment and a doctor's clinic in the center of Hamburg.

The interior, where both areas are connected, was fully redesigned to optimize the spatial limitations.

An important aim was to keep the furnishing to a minimum in order to allow the space to display its full beauty. Further open space was created by tearing down a separating wall between the library and living room. The architect wished to create a calm environment in which it was easy to concentrate on work and to enjoy the space.

Special attention was paid to the lighting, which is of great importance to Neeland and is often used as an integral part of the architecture. He believes that it has a magical quality, that it can be used to change the atmosphere completely, and that without light architecture is nothing. The rooms are mostly illuminated indirectly, for example from behind sliding window shades. The flexibility of the shades provides different dimensions of brightness, increasing the perception of space in a limited area.

Photographs: Klaus Frahm / contur

1. Shared entrance
2. Hall
3. Entrance to the dwelling
4. Living room
5. Library
6. Bedroom
7. Kitchen
8. Bathroom
9. Reception
10. Waiting-room
11. Surgery
12. Toilet
13. Photolab
14. Kitchen
15. X-ray room

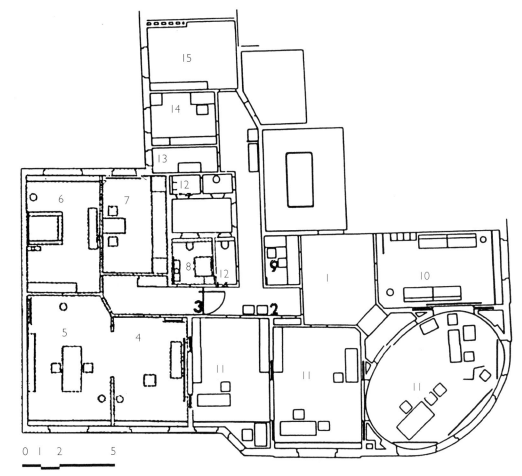

The rooms are bathed in soft light filtered through mobile panels.

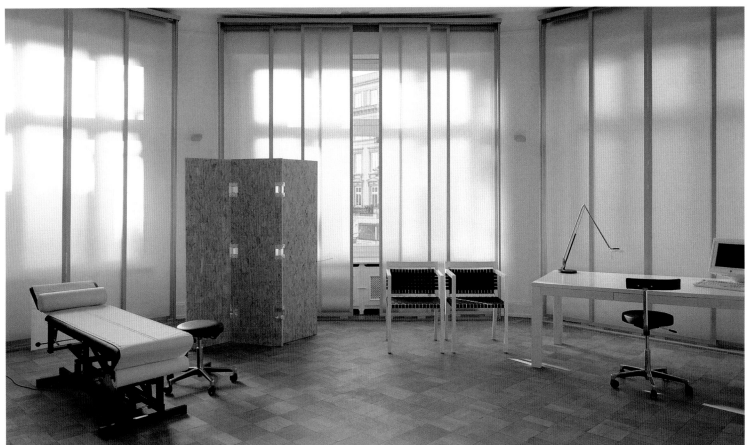

Bjarne Mastenbroek & MVRDV
Double House Utrecht

Utrecht , The Netherlands

In this Utrecht double villa the wall occupies a dominant position as a zigzagging partition between the two dwellings (and has been left in view on the exterior as a result). Paradoxically, it is virtually disregarded as a structural element.

The architects opted for a cube shape, vertically divided into two dwellings occupying a third and two thirds of the space.

To give the occupants of the smaller block a sizeable living room, the living rooms of each dwelling intrude into the volume of the other.

This gave rise to a meandering party wall that gave flexibility for the spatial organization of the villa.

The architects hark back here to building practices of times when the walls had to be structurally thick enough to allow hollows to be scooped out of them.

This villa is in effect a stacking of hollow cavities interconnected by open staircases and voids, the only enclosed areas being the bedrooms, small contained boxes suspended in space.

Almost none of the walls are positioned one above the other. Only the head elevations rise to the full height of the building. Columns were ruled out by the architects since they felt these would mar the spatial impact of the cavities. And as they wished to make the facade as transparent as possible with full-height windows, creative methods had to be devised to give the building sufficient stiffness. This play of forces was intimately resolved using pre-stressed beams, steel rods and cleverly positioned concrete balconies.

The levels in the right-hand dwelling create very fine loft-like open spaces organized in a horizontal sandwich. The left-hand dwelling is more labyrinthine. Its cavities are vertically arranged around an axis of two stacked but slightly staggered voids. From the kitchen on the ground floor the inhabitants can see right up to the roof eleven metres above.

If spatially interesting as living space, the long narrow rooms are not very practicable. For this reason, the living room on the third floor provides a welcome break from the verticality of this dwelling.

The bathroom with its fully glazed wall opens onto the roof terrace, a high parapet around the roof guaranteeing privacy though a section of it can be lowered for an unobstructed view of the park. And the roof terrace offers a permanent view of the cathedral spire.

A distinctive feature of the double villa is the façade. It is unusual in that it was not designed. The only finishing details in the facade are the sturdy wooden shuttering boards that clad the concrete sections.

Photographs: Christian Richters

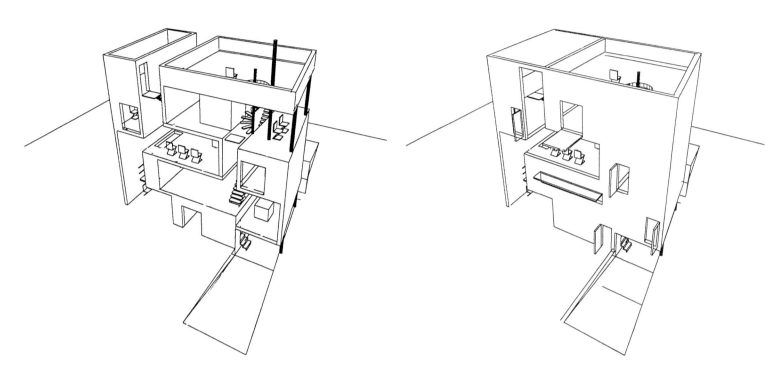

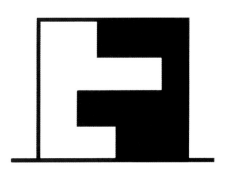

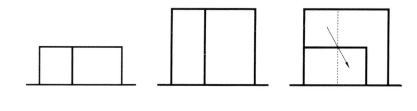

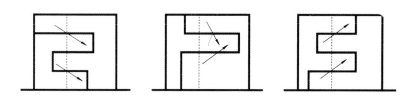

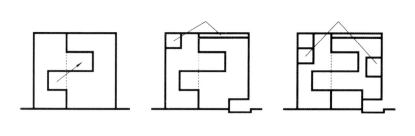

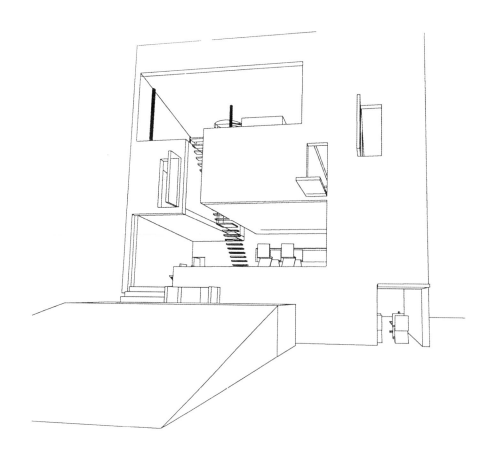

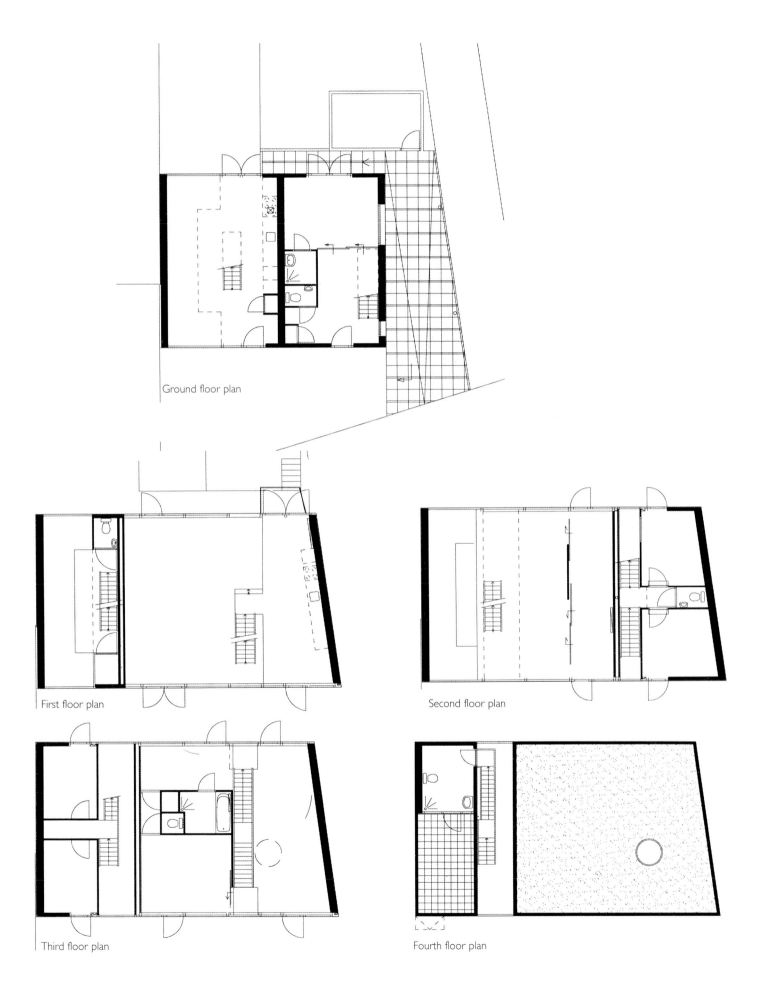

Ground floor plan

First floor plan

Second floor plan

Third floor plan

Fourth floor plan

276

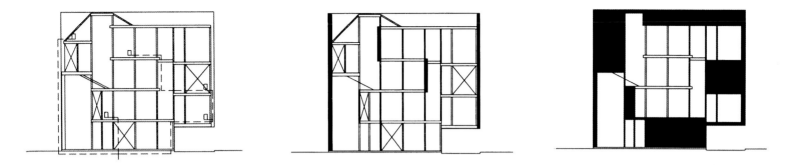

Functional schemes that show, from left to right, the drainage system, the structural stability in north-south direction and windowless facade planes.

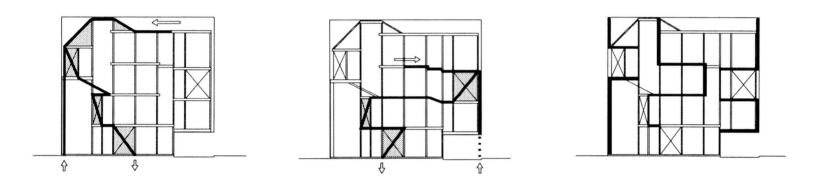

Sequence of schemes that show the general distribution of forces in the building and in the level 4 (left and center drawings) and party wall and head elevations.

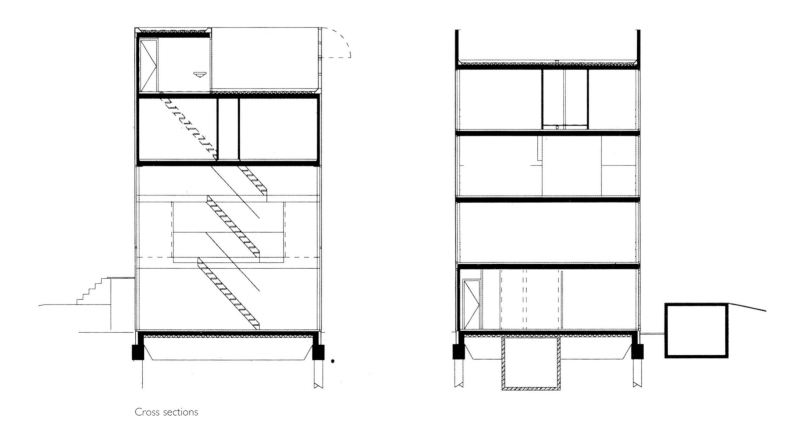

Cross sections

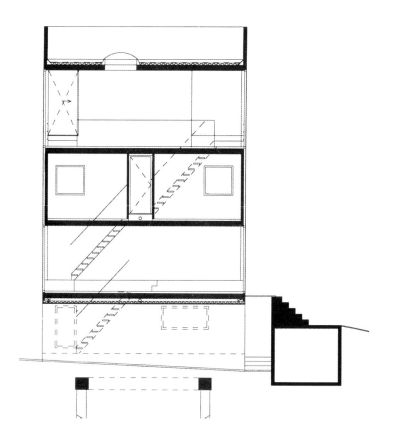

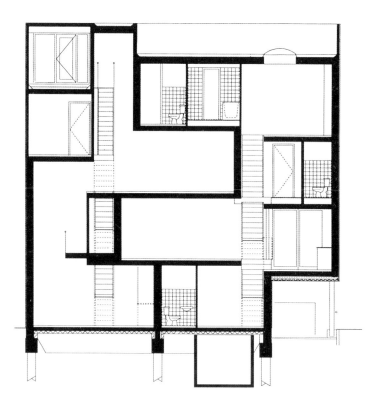

Cross sections

The interiors of both dwellings are open and diaphanous. Columns, pillars and any kind of visual obstacle were ruled out by the architects. Also, the spaces are planned as very illuminated rooms with full-height windows.

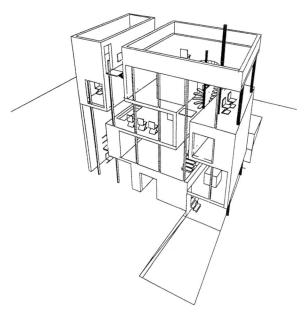

The different floors are intercommunicated by open staircases and are structured transparently, guaranteeing a flexible spatial organization.

The only closed rooms are the bedrooms, which seem to be small and surprising containers suspended in the space.

Kuth / Ranieri
Ian / Stolz Residence

San Francisco, California, USA

The house is sited on a narrow alley that changes from street to garden at the building's front door. The project falls between the grid of the city and the organic nature of a garden landscape. Views from the house include the Golden Gate Bridge and the hills of Marin beyond. The plans at each floor are organized to remain as open as possible to these views, with the central living zones bracketed by support areas, such as stairs and bathrooms, to either side.

Like the plan, the facade responds to the context through the transformation of common typological elements specific to the Bay Area (for example, bay window, front facing garage door and street-side roof deck).

These elements are folded into a synthetic assembly of clear sealed mahogany panels and ledges. Again, returning to the siting of the project it was the goal of the architects to propose an architecture that fused the different orders of city, garden and building into a singular system.

Included in the project was a new laminated glass garden wall, strategically placed at the south side of the building where the main floor opens to an adjacent garden.

The challenge was two-fold: to provide privacy to the occupants and to reframe the landscape. Like the garden beyond, the wall is a volume filled with light and shade. In the daytime, the glass is illuminated by an internal lamping that infuses the entire wall, patio, and rooms of the house with an iridescent sheen.

Photographs: T. Sakashita

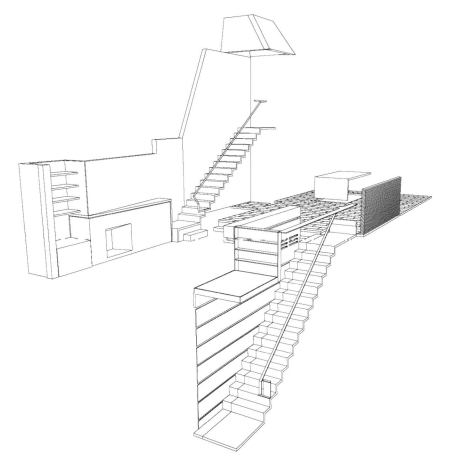

Site plan

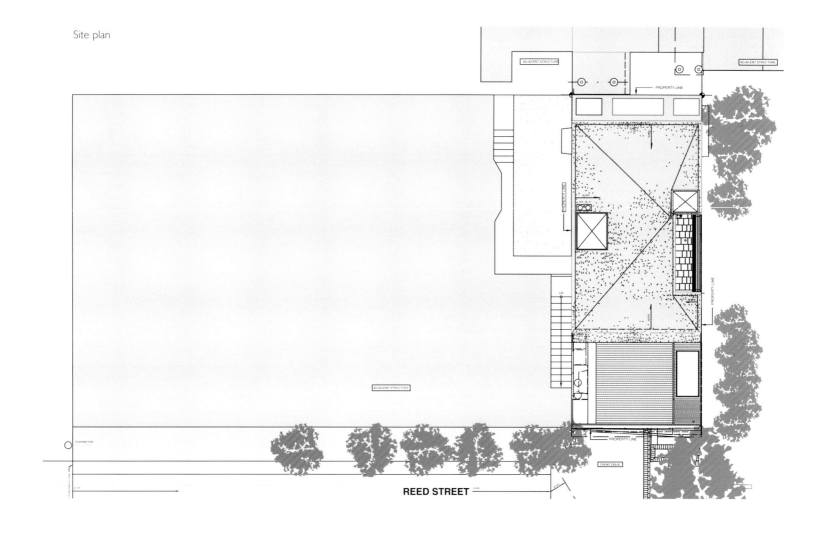

REED STREET

Railing detail

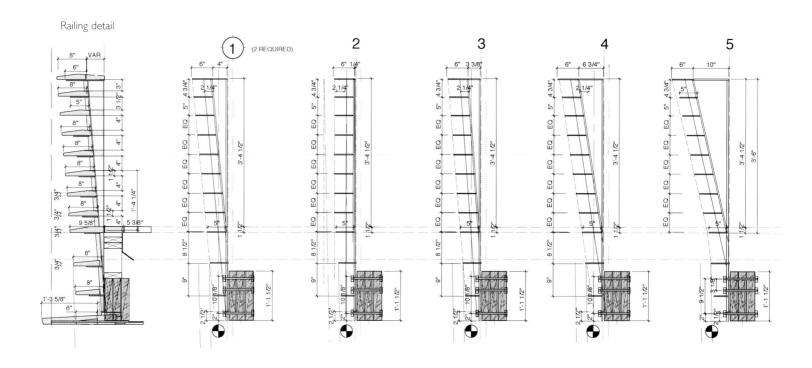

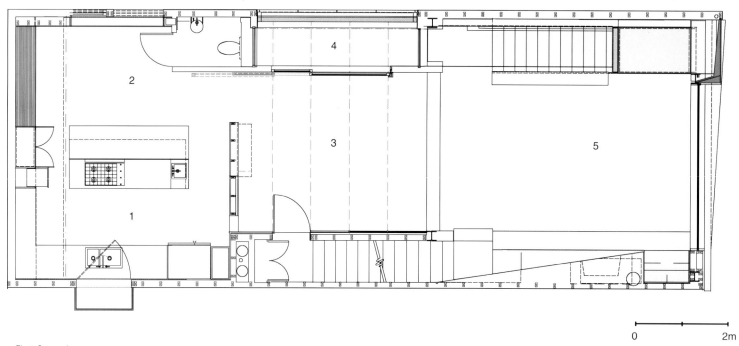

First floor plan
1. Kitchen 2. Breakfast 3. Dining room 4. Patio 5. Living room

0 ———— 2m

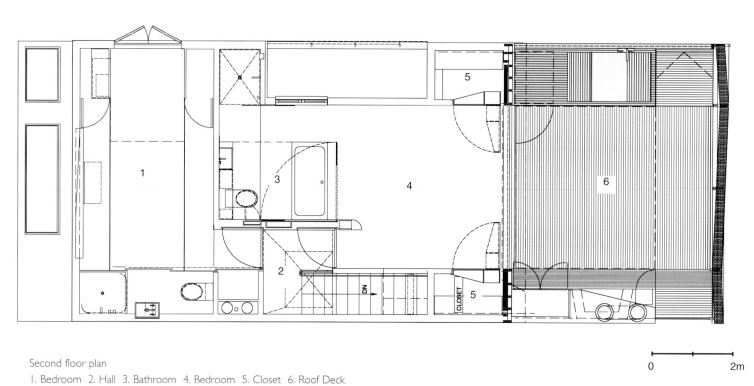

Second floor plan
1. Bedroom 2. Hall 3. Bathroom 4. Bedroom 5. Closet 6. Roof Deck

0 ———— 2m

Guest and master bedroom suites are contiguous volumes that spill into the outdoor roof deck where a hot-tub and fireplace overlook the Golden Gate Bridge. The bathrooms have been placed to one side of the plan in order to create unobstructed central living spaces.

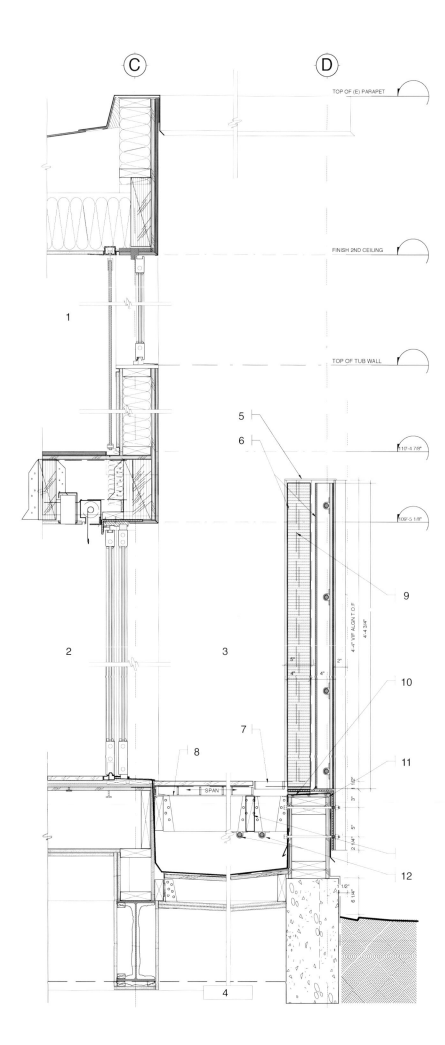

TOP OF (E) PARAPET

FINISH 2ND CEILING

TOP OF TUB WALL

110'-4 7/8"

109'-5 1/8"

SPAN

The windows devised for this project are a thoroughly modern approach to the bay window so typical of this area's architecture.

Constructive section

1. Master bath
2. Dining room / Comedor
3. Exterior patio / Patio exterior
4. Basement / Sótano
5. Steel cap / Casquete de acero
6. 1/4" flange / Ala de 1/4"
7. Aluminim grating access panel
8. Aluminim grating to hold stone patio
9. 1/4" stacked glass (4"x6'-0" laminated)
10. Stainless steel shims
11. Water proofing membrane and metal flashing
12. 3/4" rope light fed through rigid plastic tube for support between joists

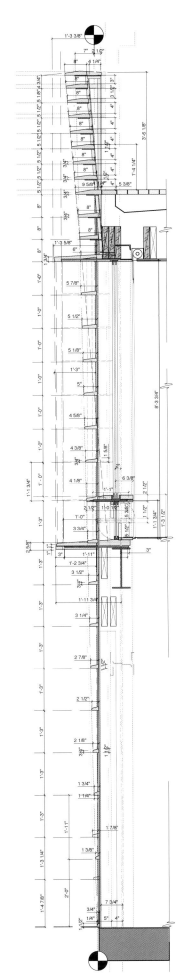

Facade section

Daniele Marques & Bruno Zurkirchen
Haus Kraan Lang

Emmembrücke, Switzerland

The plot for which the single-family dwelling was to be designed is located in an area with a heterogeneous planning situation, a zone of agglomeration in which the urban fabric gives way to the countryside. Buildings of varying uses populate the vicinity: farm buildings, cubic zigzag apartment blocks built in the sixties, and in a concrete single-family dwelling.

The aim of the architectural design was to respond to the planning regulations by means of two floors consisting of an ephemeral container in opposition to the more solid neighboring constructions. Both floors are south facing.

The living area opens onto a covered veranda, the top of which is slightly lower than the top of the sliding windows, thus allowing a strip of natural light to enter the living space. The north side is closed in order to shut off unwanted views of the nearby railway line.

The position of the container, in exact relation to the neighboring concrete single-family dwelling, is intended to define an exterior space belonging to both houses. The single-family dwelling is prefabricated, the construction system being based on large panels for light constructions and pillars resting on a pedestal in the basement. It is covered with untreated trapezoidal aluminum sheet. This aluminum cladding was used for all the exterior surfaces, including the roof. The remaining wooden constructional elements were left untreated, except for a wax coating.

Photographs: Daniel Mayer

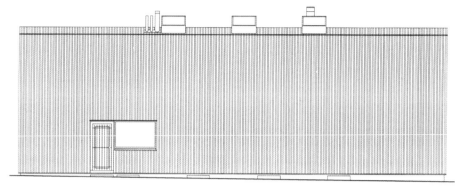

North elevation

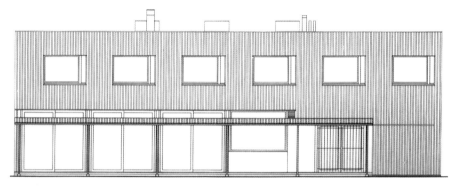

South elevation

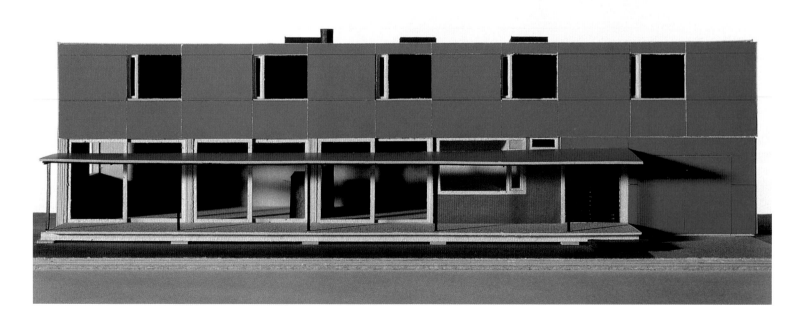

First floor plan

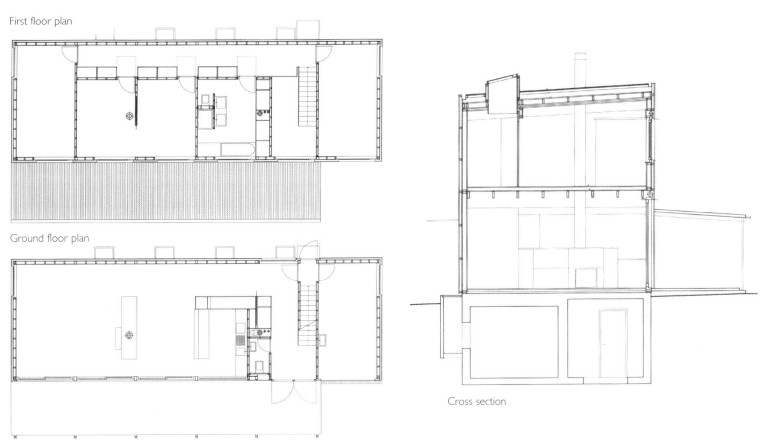

Ground floor plan

Cross section

289

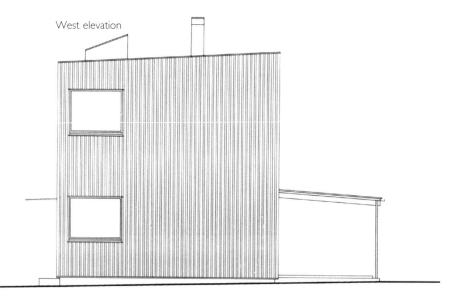

West elevation

G. Hamonic et J.C. Masson
House in a Garage

Paris, France

When a couple with children who are fond of ample space and contemporary design decide to free themselves from the corset of a Haussman building in Paris and are allergic to ready-to-wear real estate, they must take a decision on architecture. And with the same impetus they must offer the project to young designers. In life, the success of a project is often a question of confidence.

The chain that was established during this operation between the customer, the architect and the contractor is the illustration of this. Conquered from nothing, or almost nothing, this domestic dwelling was created from scratch from the first sketch to handover in a full year. The investment of the architects was proportionate to the confidence that the customers placed in them.

And this is how this old shell opening onto a passage on the outskirts of the old section of Paris became the mansion of their dreams. The scheme was not, strictly speaking, a rehabilitation but a more radical intervention, a way of making full use of the plot.

Two different environments are woven together: on the passage side, the old houses are preserved, with their roofing and their loft. In the heart of the block, in the place of the old hangar, the fluid space of the new intervention expands.

The house takes the old dimensions of the shell (192 m² floor space, 6 m height to the base of the roof), crossed by a court (3 m x 6 m) that regulates the party wall facing the court with a light partition. The 18 m2 of space planted with bamboo becomes a garden, a source of light and a horizon of vegetation for all the rooms.

Preserving its original character, the facade on the dead-end is almost unaltered. This choice of discretion and respect for the surrounding fabric that was desired from the first drawings by the architects helped the inhabitants of this modest dead-end of old Paris to accept the scheme.

On crossing the threshold, the visitor is inhaled toward a large, extremely open volume (the living room), which opens onto the court. The scenario of daily life is thus discovered. It forms a continuous whole of which full use is made, and life moves into the hollows of the works. The different spaces are linked by the interplay of light and the contrast of volumes. No doors, no obstacles. Transitions take the form of delicate filters: a bamboo hedge in the court, a set of transparent or translucent polycarbonate screens for the kitchen, dining area, lounge and offices.

Photographs: Hervé Abbadie / Hamonic + Masson Architectes

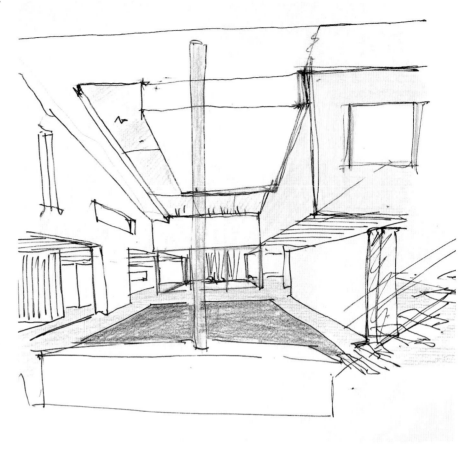

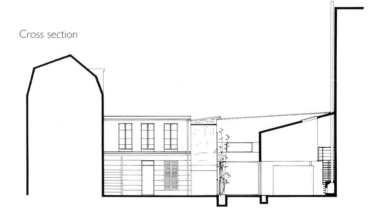

Cross section

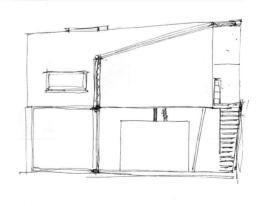

N

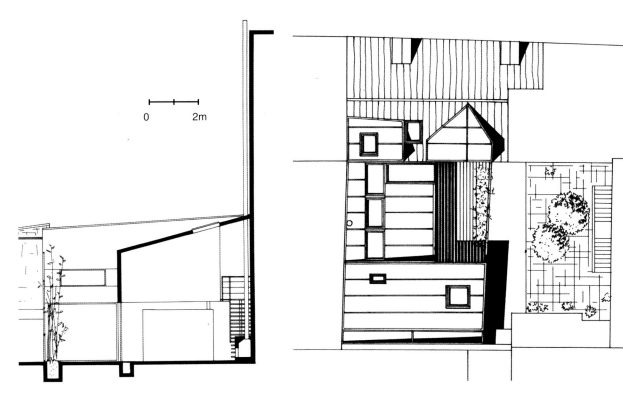

0   2m

Site plan

Ground floor plan

11

10

12

9

8

7

6

5

4

3

2

1

0   2m

1. Entry
2. Access to children's room
3. Laundry
4. WC
5. Video
6. Kitchen
7. Dining room
8. Room
9. Access to parent's room
10. Library
11. Office
12. Terrace

In fitting out the dwelling the architects avoided any mannerism in the materials, using only what was essential for the house to breathe: a metal structure, white or colored partitions, transparencies.

First floor plan

Existing floor

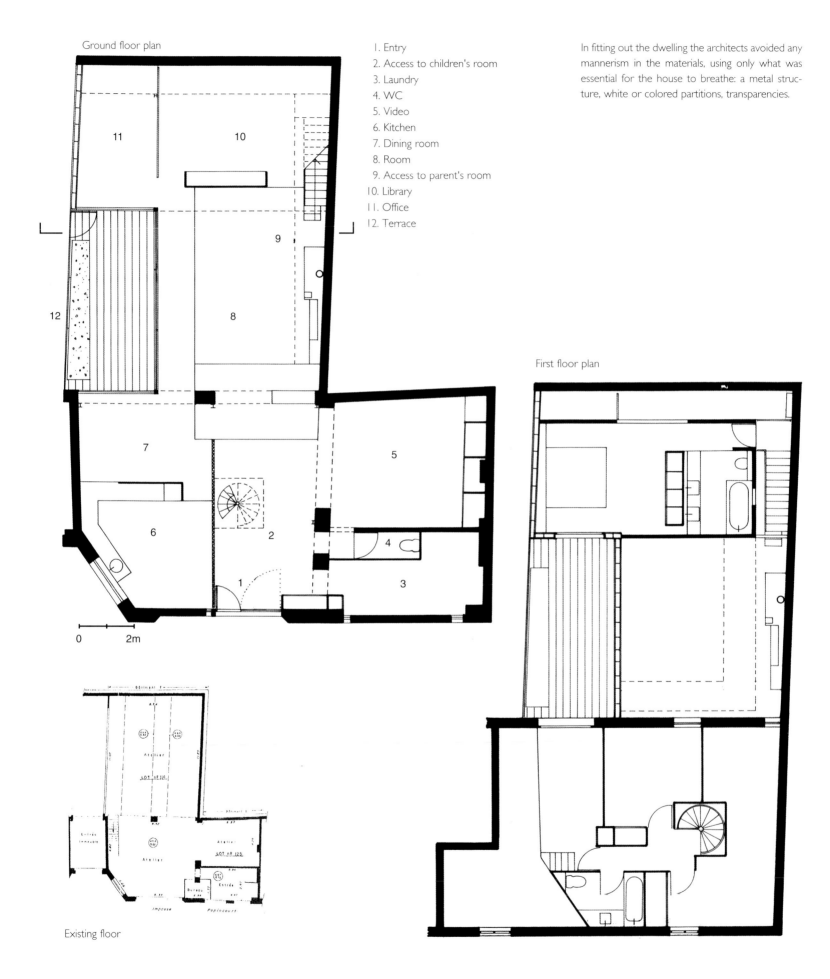

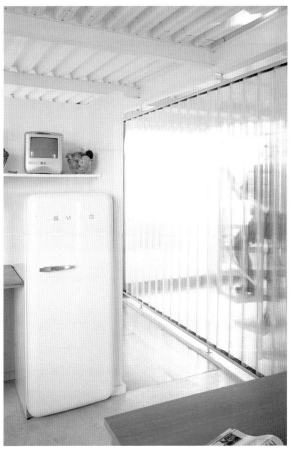

Rather than a plot locked amid many buildings, this new place of life breathes vitality soaked in omnipresent natural lighting.

Construction detail

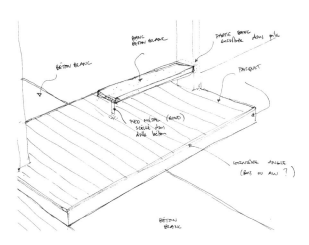

Eugeen Liebaut
Verhaeghe House

Sint Pieters Leeuw, Belgium

The program for this house near Brussels was chosen from among ten competing architectural studios. The Verhaeghe house is a simple two-story structure with a flat roof, hemmed in on both sides by neighboring buildings. Since the site itself was seven meters wide and zoning restrictions would only allow a height of six meters, a modest volume had to be designed.

With such spatial restrictions, the architects decided to make room by sinking the ground floor 80cm to the level of the foundation masonry. Financially, this is a simple enough operation; while the advantages gained in spatial configuration are highly attractive.

The living room is a high-ceilinged, transparent space. Here, the inhabitants move freely about between two strategically-placed volumes - the kitchen and the toilet - which do not reach the full height of the ceiling. Together, these volumes form a screen of sorts within the transparent volume which provides the necessary privacy from the public street. The high and wide glass facade rises from an incision between the volume and the socle like a rare and floating object.

The rear facade is also entirely glazed, making the steel-grated terrace outside seem like a continuation of the dwelling. By working with grates, the bedrooms on the ground floor are ensured sufficient light. This relatively small house enjoys a spatiality which many a majestic villa can only dream of.

Photographs: Saskia Vanderstichele

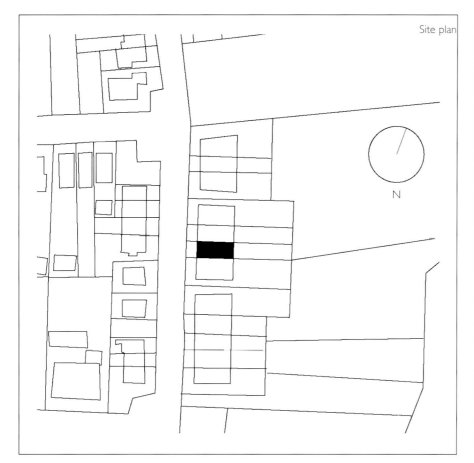

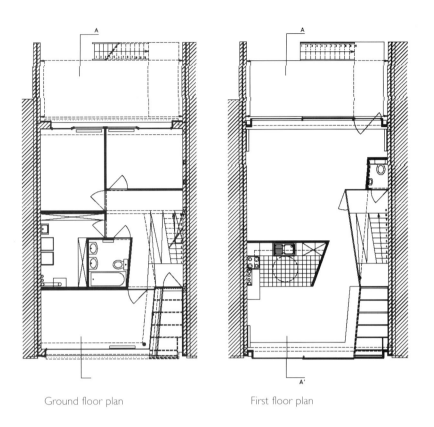

Ground floor plan   First floor plan

Since zoning restrictions required a height of no more than 6 meters, interior space was gained by sinking the house by nearly one meter.

The block containing the kitchen is positioned to shield the interior from views from the street.

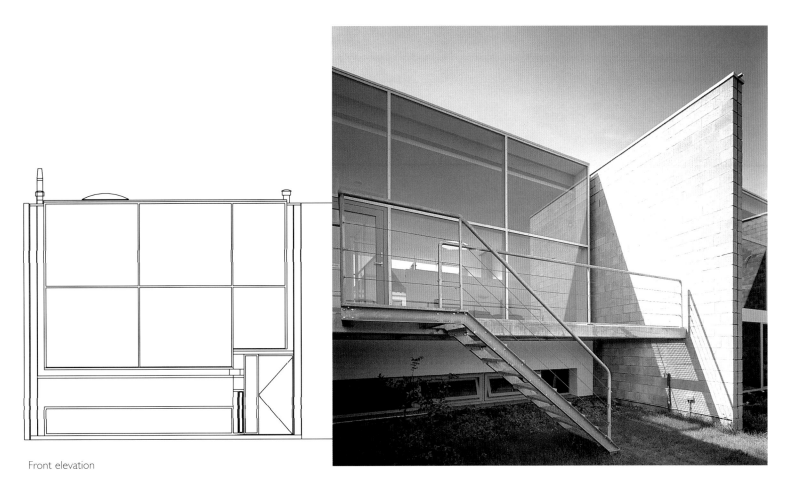

Front elevation

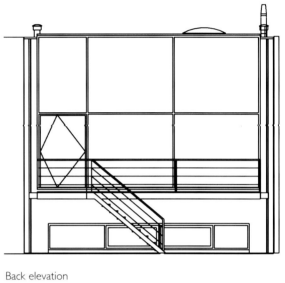

Back elevation

Sir Norman Foster & Partners
Private House

Germany

This is a house for a young family with small children. The building is sited on a southfacing slope, well wooded and with fine views to the valley beyond.

Access to the site from the road is directly on to the roof terrace of the house which is a two story concrete and brickwork structure dug into the hillside. From this level an entrance ramp leads down through the levels of the house to the lower garden terrace.

Both of these outdoor spaces are protected by a louvered roof with its own independent steel structure.

The lowest level is the family domain which contains the book-lined hearth and the open kitchen. Both areas are adjacent to the double height living space. One of the features of the house is its splendid kitchen. The owner has a personal interest in cooking which is reflected in the professional equipment and tools with a very efficient extraction system.

All levels of the dwelling are connected by exterior steps in the landscape. These allow direct access to the garden for children, quiet outdoor spaces related to the parents study and a private front door for the maid.

The design, based on an unusual combination of inside and outside circulation enables the house to offer the family and their friends an unusual degree of community as well as respecting the privacy of the individuals.

Photographs: Dennis Gilbert

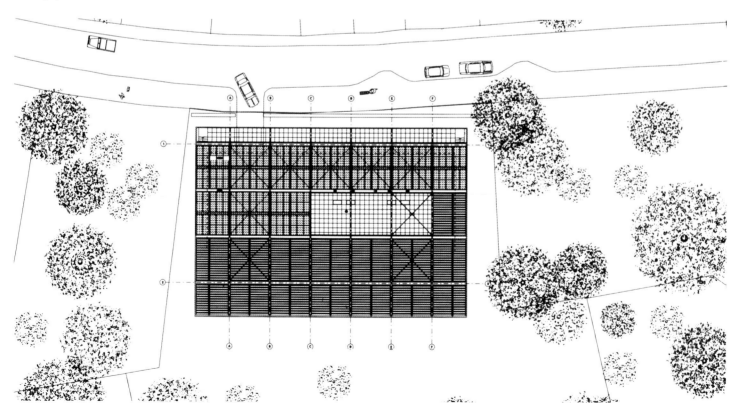

Second floor plan

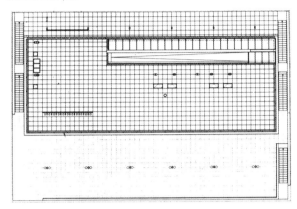

First floor plan

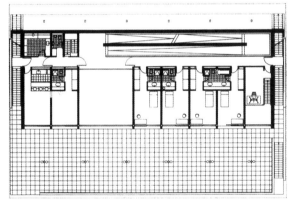

Ground floor plan

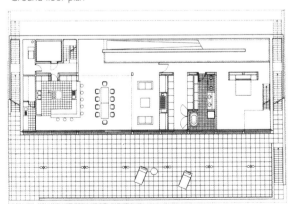

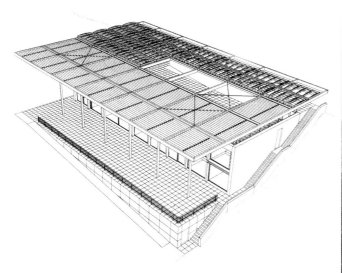

The external appearance of the building is dominated by a large lattice supported by an independent metal structure.

North elevation

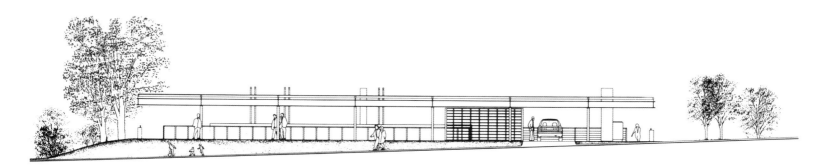

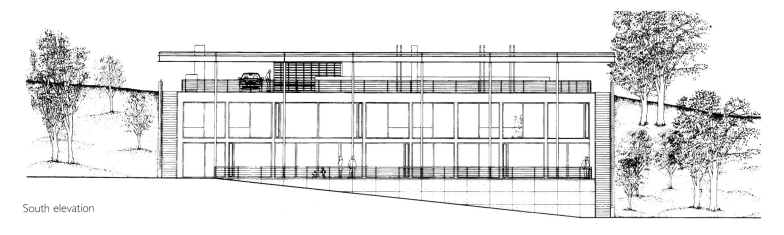

South elevation

Jun Aoki
House I

Tokyo, Japan

The most has been made of this relatively small plot. Of the 61 m^2 of available ground space, a two-story home with a basement has been built on just 37 m^2 (the total floor area is 109 m^2). However, its impact on the surrounding neighborhood cannot be judged by its size alone. The eye-catching and unexpected geometry of the facade sets this home apart from the rest.

The project is a sculpted concrete shell placed in the space between two existing houses. Broadly speaking, the structure is comprised of two independent volumes placed within the shell. The upper floor, from which is seemingly suspended a glass-enclosed mezzanine overlooking the dining room, comprise the first volume; the second is made up of the ground floor, which encloses the basement space.

The primary structural system is of reinforced concrete. The facades are clad in wood paneling, with windows framed in aluminum and steel.

In the interior, the sleek, modern look of steel and concrete competes with the homey warmth of wood. High and wide expanses of exposed concrete slabs make an imposing wall cladding. The floors are done almost entirely in unstained wood throughout the home, the only exception being the unique flooring material used in the mezzanine: leather.

Painted steel stairways and handrails, and custom-designed steel cabinets are the elements which provide the necessary dark visual counterweight to the light tones of concrete and unstained wood.

Photographs: Tsunejiro Watanabe

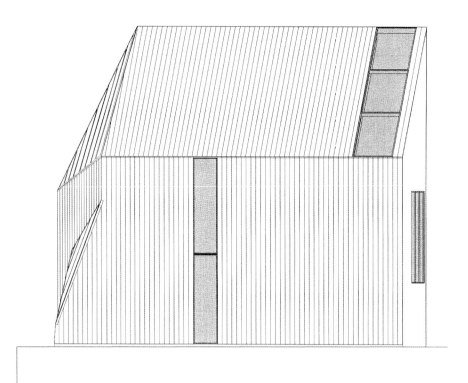

West elevation

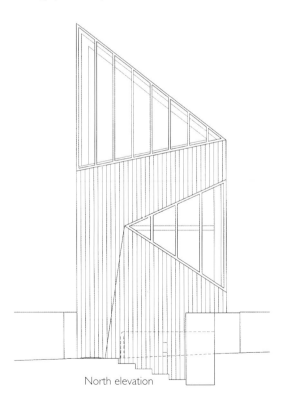

North elevation

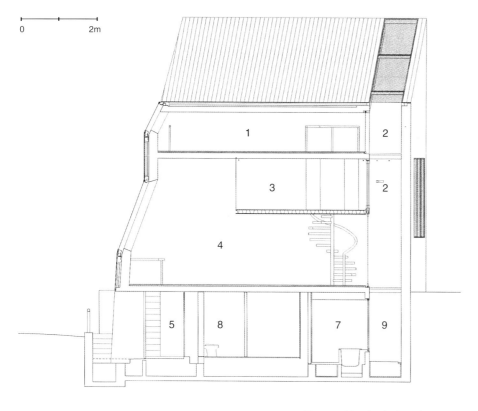
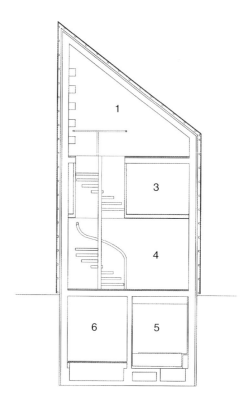

Cross and longitudinal sections

1. Study
2. Terrace
3. Bedroom
4. Kitchen
5. Entrance
6. Storage
7. Bathroom
8. WC
9. Areaway

The walls are clad in high and wide expanses of exposed concrete. The floors are done almost entirely in unstained wood, the only exception being the unique flooring material used in the mezzanine: leather.

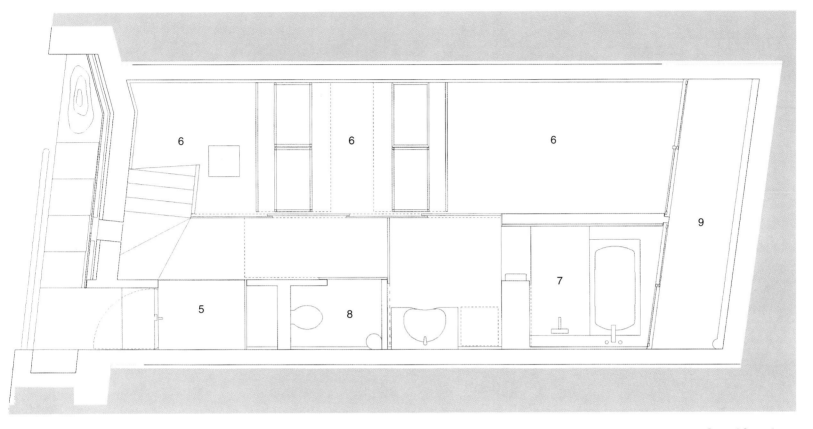

Ground floor plan

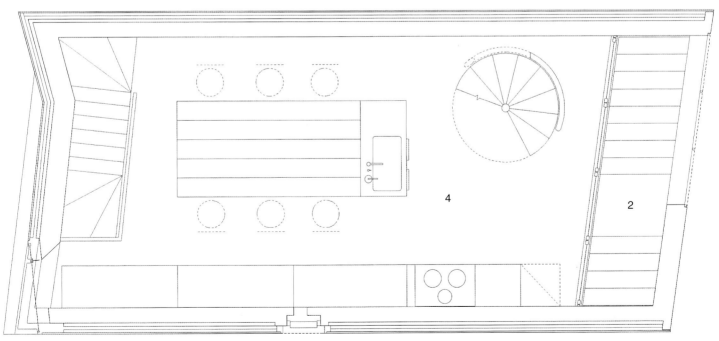

First floor plan

319

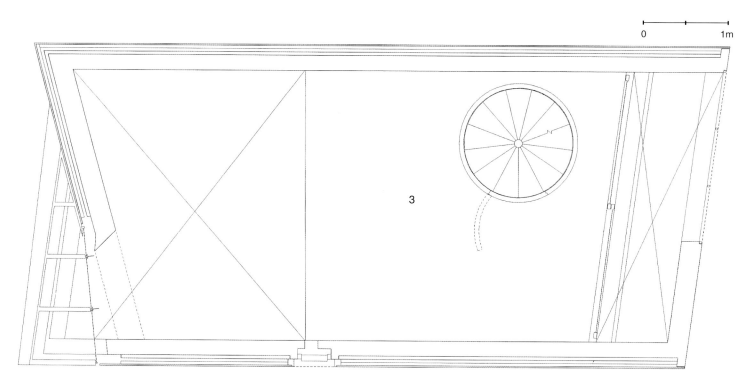

Mezzanine

1. Study   2. Terrace   3. Bedroom

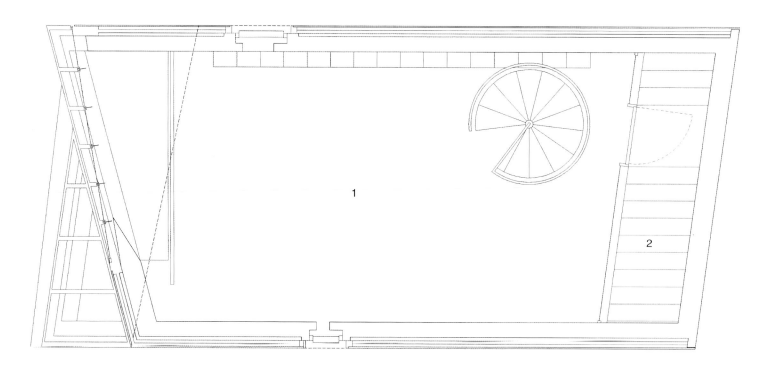

Second floor plan

Marin-Trottin
(Péripheriqués Architectes)
MR House

Pompone, France

Stretched along a strip of marshy land in the Seine and Marne region, this metal-frame house seems to form part of the landscape. The dwelling slopes with the 15% drop in land level and is camouflaged by greenery, while the painted panels of the façade blend with the garden. Huge windows frame the lower and upper gardens, thus highlighting the relationship between interior and exterior. As a final touch, small shutters allow the fresh scent of the garden to waft into the home.

The tight, narrow plot of 17 meters in length gave rise to an elongated design which has the advantage of reducing the building's visual impact on the garden. By the same token, this strip-form creates an historical link with the farming activity that used to take place on the site. The rooms unfold along the slope, from the living room to the bedroom. Both public and private spaces are conceived as half-stories so as to be in close contact with the garden at all times.

Intended as a follow-up to design work undertaken for the "36 Proposals for a Home" project, this scheme illustrates the designers' ambition to make an architect-designed house for basically the same price as a pre-fab home, while ensuring that it meshes subtly with its surroundings.

Photographs: Hervé Abbadie

The sequence on the opposite page illustrates the inspiration behind the design of the façades. The colored panels were based on a pixilated abstraction of a garden and represent the natural variations in color tone and intensity of light.

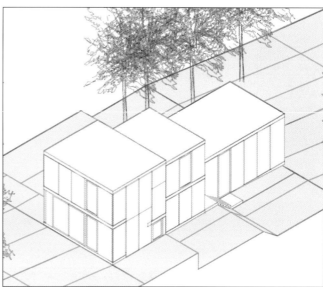

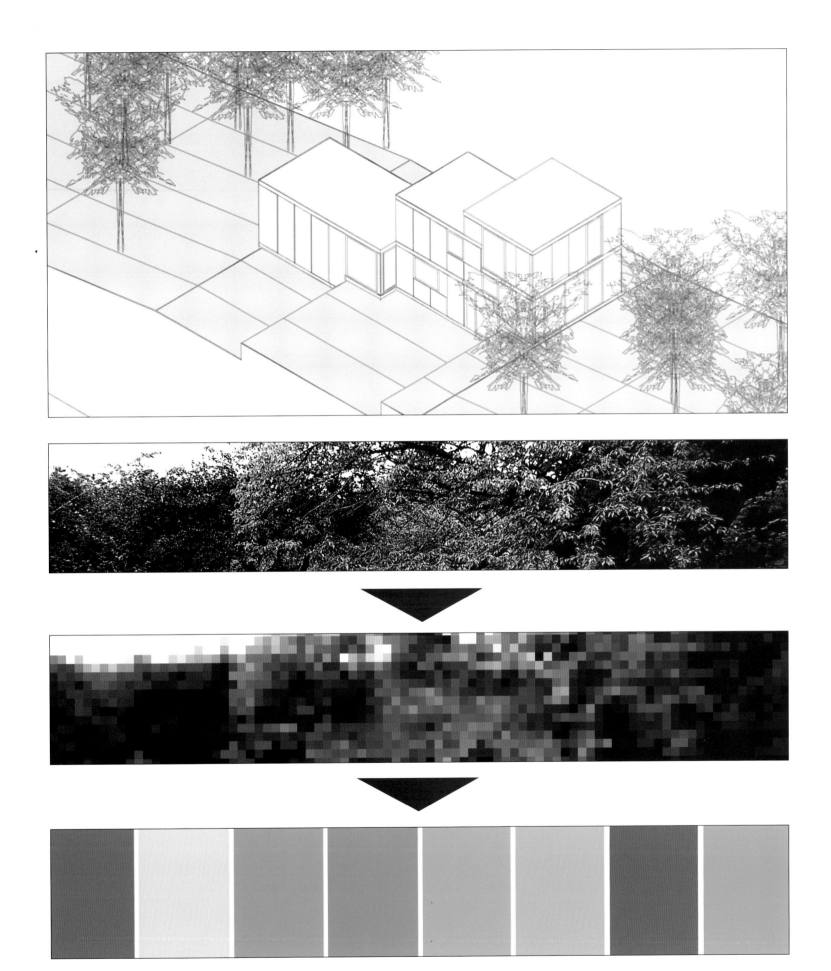

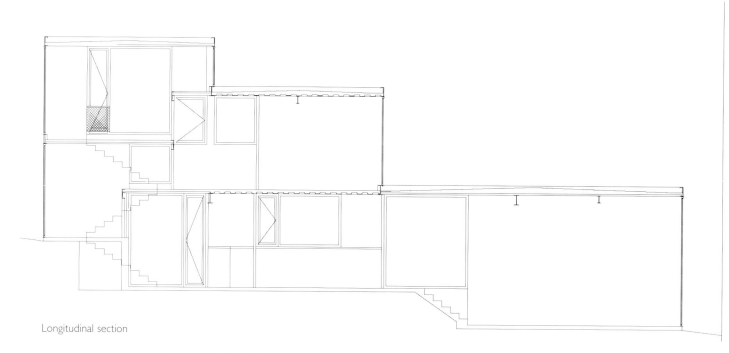

Longitudinal section

The sketches of the four façades illustrate how the designers made every effort to adapt the design scheme to the natural lay of the land, thus adding a great deal of variation in an otherwise uniform, rectangular ground plan.

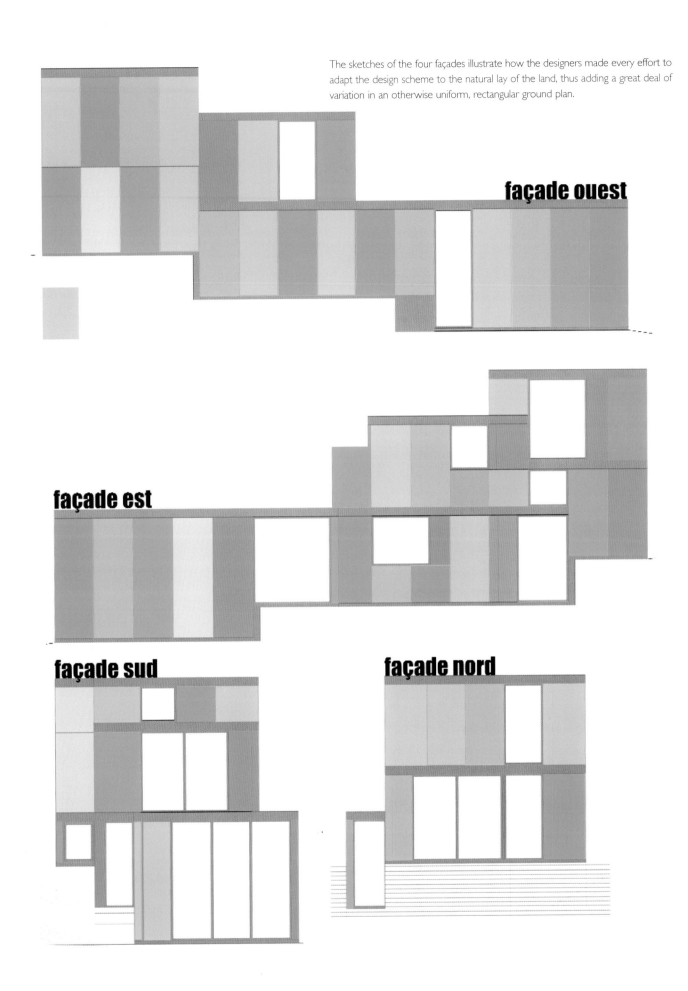

façade ouest

façade est

façade sud

façade nord

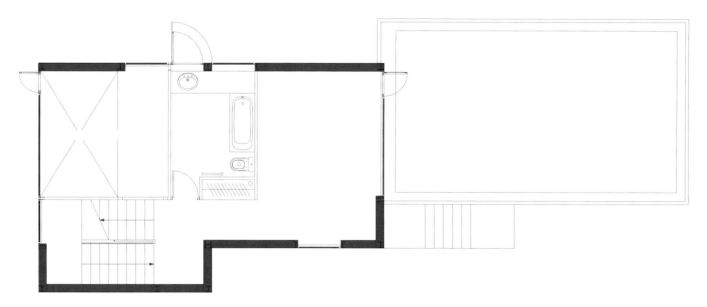

First floor plan

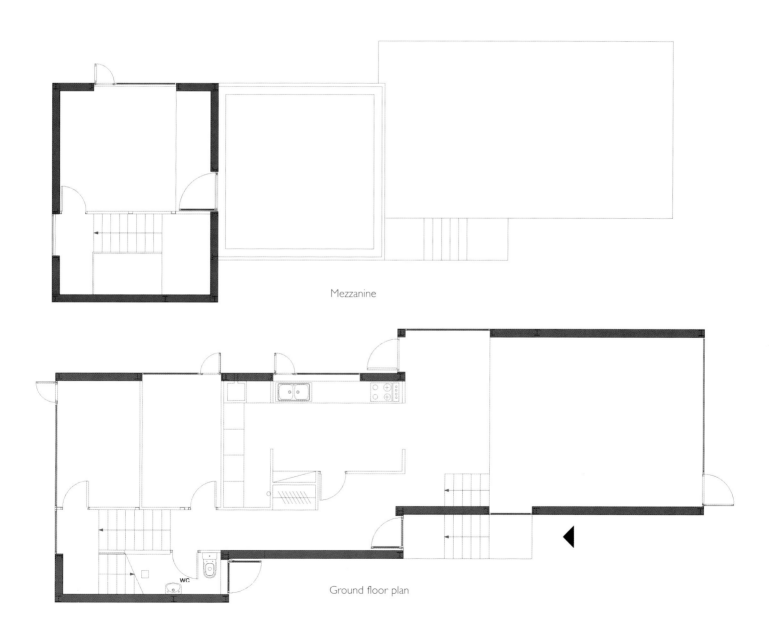

Mezzanine

Ground floor plan

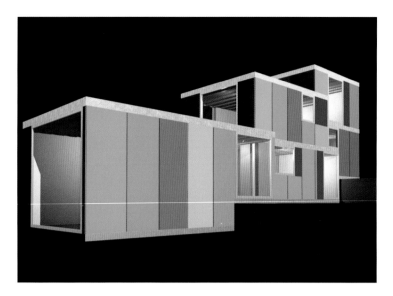

The rooms unfold along the slope, from the living room to the bedroom. Both public and private spaces are conceived as half-stories so as to be in close contact with the garden at all times.

Benson & Forsyth
Marico House

London, UK

Located in Islington on the north bank of the Grand Union Canal, the site consisted of the shell of a derelict factory and two cottages. The single-story walls of the canal towpath and the gardens to the north, together with the two-story cottage walls which face the park and the existing houses, have been retained.

Within the house a metal valley-roof supported on perforated metal troughs and a steel frame is carried centrally on two pairs of steel columns. Externally the roof is reminiscent of a traditional Islington valley-roof, while internally it reads as a free-standing umbrella dissociated from the perimeter walls and independent of the galleries and volumes below.

The ground floor is occupied by the principal living spaces, which relate to the studio across the courtyard, or internally through the single-story dining/conference room, which may be used in conjunction with both the studio and the living floor.

The first-floor gallery contains a second living space: a dressing room and bedroom which overlook the park and the canal and extend on to the roof terrace over the single-story link into the office gallery within the studio.

The upper floor is composed of two cubes: the bathroom within a 2.1 meter cube made of opal white glass, and the main bedroom, which is located in a roof-lit enclosure suspended over the lower sitting area.

The design of the workshop section was governed by the need to maintain the two-story enclosure of the adjacent buildings on the canal side and to keep the level of the roof below the single-story wall of the gardens on the north. The roof and all of the wall planes are dissociated by glazing which washes the planes with indirect light.

Photographs: Hélène Binet

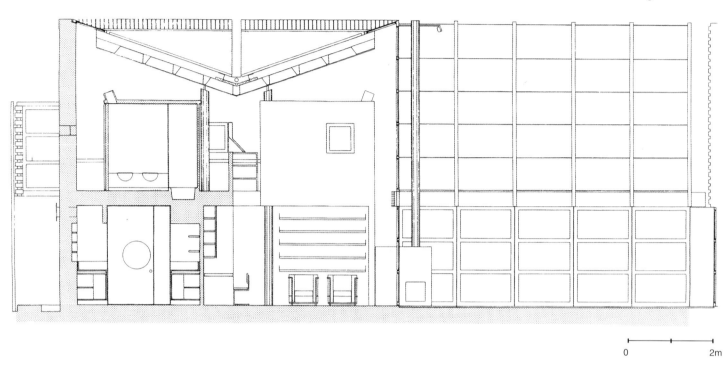

0   2m

Ground floor plan

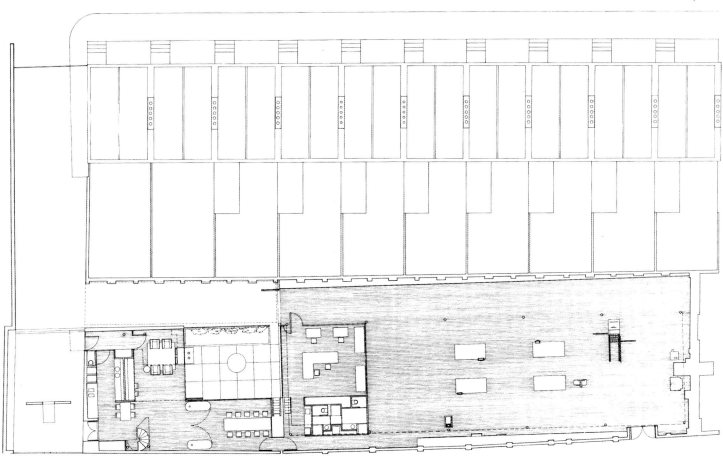

First floor plan

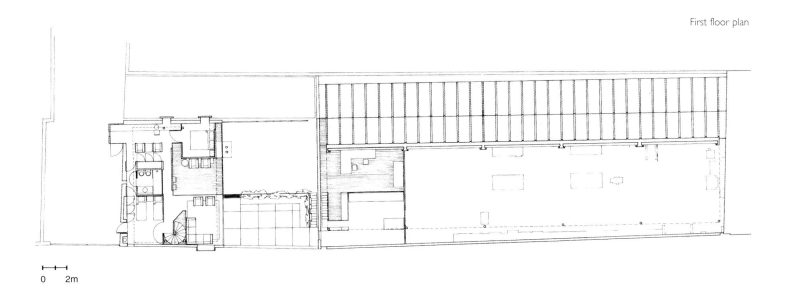

0   2m

337

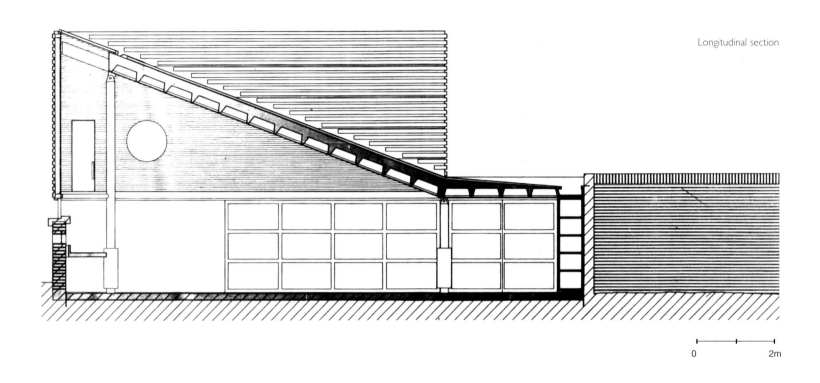

Longitudinal section

0   2m

Mathias Klotz
Ugarte House

Maitencillo, Chile

Casa Ugarte is a small wooden refuge, a weekend house located at the edge of the Maitencillo Sur cliff, 150 kilometers north of the Chilean capital.

The building consists of two wooden volumes in two levels, connected by a sort of gallery, also of double height, that organizes the access and articulates the interior spaces.

A strict geometry defines the architecture of this close and serene building, located in a strong and infinite landscape. The smaller volume houses the bedrooms and bathrooms, while the larger one houses the public areas, such as the kitchen, the dining room and the living room, all on the first floor. There is a small room designed to house a study located on the second floor of the main building. This space is located over the living room whose south front is also glazed and looks to the splendid sea views.

The terraces have been designed as semi-built spaces. They are parts that have been cut out of the volumes in order to protect them from the strong south winds. This means that, in particular, the larger volume has a great void on the south side, giving continuity to the living room and extending the spatial perception of the interior.

Wood plays a leading role among the materials used. Tongue and groove boards have been used for the outer cladding and wooden panels for the inner cladding. Outside, the wood has been painted in white.

In this strict and rigorous geometry, the architect has experimented with wood to gain an ornamental interplay of patterns: the smaller volume was clad vertically, whereas the larger one was clad horizontally, a technique which also accentuates the individuality of each one.

Photographs: Alberto Piovano

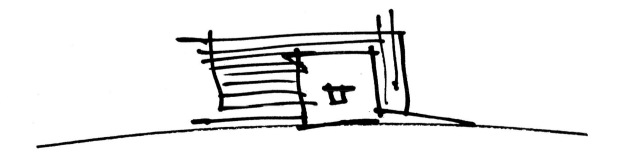

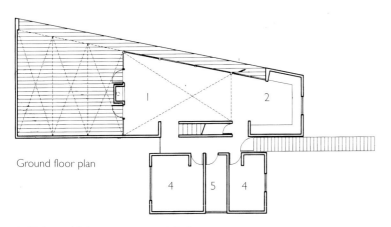

Ground floor plan

1. Dining and living room
2. Kitchen
3. Study

4. Bedroom
5. Bathroom
6. Master bedroom

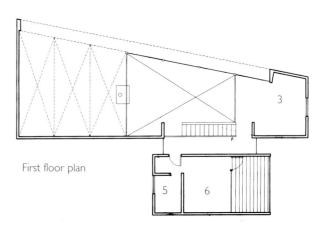

First floor plan

The terrace located at the south end of the western façade was designed as a semi-built space to protect it from the strong south winds.

The furnishings in the interiors are simple and functional, most of them made in Italy, except the custom-made table in the living-room, designed by the architect.

343

Mario Botta
House in Montagnola

Montagnola, Switzerland

The architecture of Mario Botta is characterized by its formal power and the strong presence of its volumes. His buildings do not attempt to blend into their surroundings; rather, they aim to impose themselves on them, to implant themselves with all the vigor of their architectural mass and become landmarks in the landscape. This single-family dwelling is a clear example of this tendency. Located in the Swiss canton of Ticino, it is not subordinated to its Alpine setting. Instead, it takes advantage of the relief of the setting to emerge with force from the site, seeking to make a plastic, expressive impact.

This project bases its formal strength on volume. The building rises out of the ground to form a large semicylindrical body.

The curve of the outer wall is interrupted by a large glazed area which is set back from the principal plane. These windows flood the house with light and open it up to views of the valley. A row of bull's-eyes along the top introduce a nautical idiom into the Alpine context.

A longitudinal body housing the leisure facilities (swimming pools, sauna and gym) and a large garage were attached to the main volume, taking advantage of the slope.

Photographs: Pino Musi

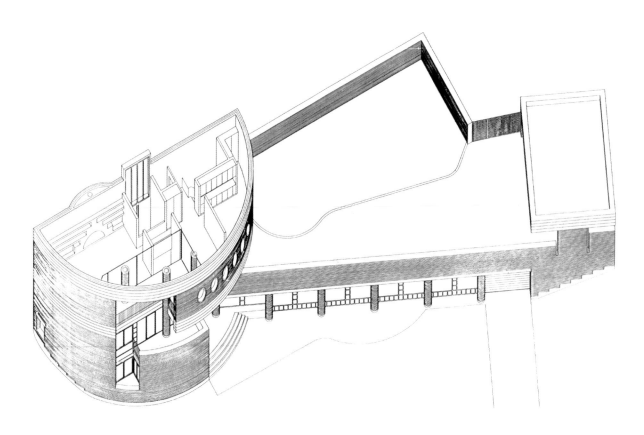

Site plan

Ground floor plan

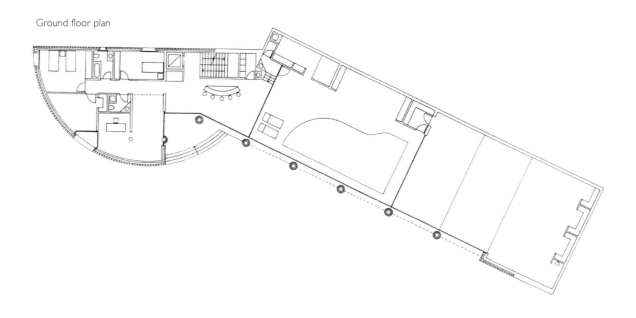

First floor plan

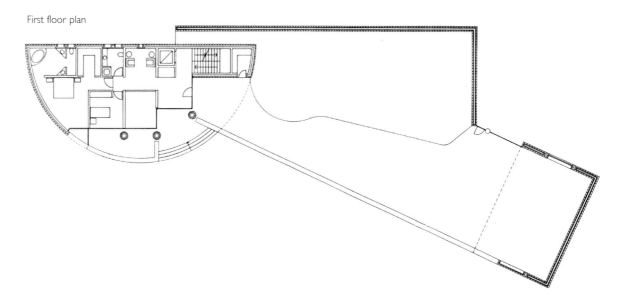

Second floor plan

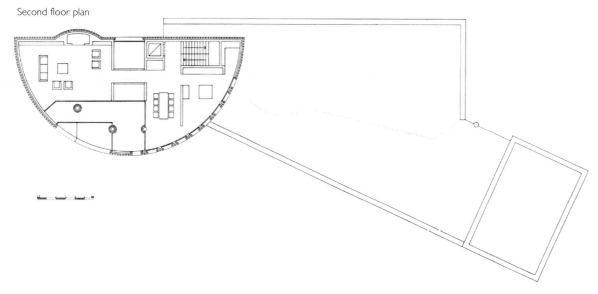

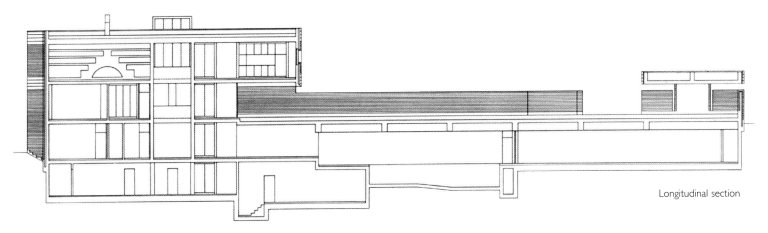

Longitudinal section

Ushida Findlay Partnership
Soft and Hairy House

Tsukuba, Japan

We were contacted by a young couple who were both architectural journalists. Intrigued by the provocative statements of Salvador Dalí on the architecture of the future, they requested a house which was soft and hairy.

More than a flight of fantasy, it was their attempt to link and affiliate spaces of different forms and contexts. It was an appropriation of surrealism, which released them from the socially cohesive, normative view of housing development in Japan.

In typology a hairy surface is one in which the continuity properties of surfaces are studied through flows. We read the request for the "soft and hairiness" to be a mixture. Theirs was not a purely esoteric desire; rather it was radical, polemic and political.

The form of the house embodies the couple, his head and her head face each other across the entryway and their child lies between. The internal plan is a landscape of the familiar and unifamiliar.

Of all the arts, architecture has been the most distant from surrealism because of its realistic economic basis. Even rare examples of surrealist architecture such as the Beistegui apartment by Corbusier and Casa Maraparte by Libera, seem to be client instigated.

Surrealism was an attempt to overcome "reality" framed by the illusions of nationality, currency, culture and community. This was achieved by liberating and sharing individual illusions by referring to psychoanalysis and Marxism by means such as dream / insanity and automatism.

In the status quo where "reality" goes beyond our imagination and obscures the boundary between real and virtual, we often see images derived from surrealist art occurring into our daily lives. In other words, the "real" is copying art. In order to solve the problems of the house building type -in this kind of status quo - it is effective to make a space / container of life floating in between the "virtual"- private illusion / subconsciousness and "real" economical and social substance of architecture. Conventional methods of architecture never addressed these problems.

Dali's enormous body of work is recognised as a materialisation of dream. If Japanese minimalist design, the currently dominant architectural force, purports to "de-materialize the real" our attempt may be called a "materialisation of dream" in the manner of Dalí. We tried to envisage a "reality" which can exist by scattering decoded architectural and non-architectural elements in one space. Inside a concrete tube spiralling around a courtyard a blue egg-shaped bathroom and amorphous blue stone-inscribed "dream" "dread" and "desire" float in the space. A strange tactility pervades the interior; its walls are swathed in canvas, a door is wrapped in fake fur, and a hairy foliage overhangs. But this new "reality" somehow has a vague periphery as it has slipped off from the real "real" of the outside world.

Photographs: Katsuhisa Kida

Site plan

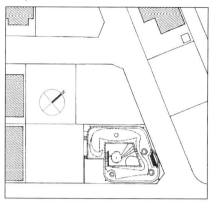

The foliage occupying the entire roof of this dwelling spills out over delicately curved walls. Inside, the building displays the complexity and beauty of organic forms in all of the spaces, which are arranged so as to receive the light from the central patio.

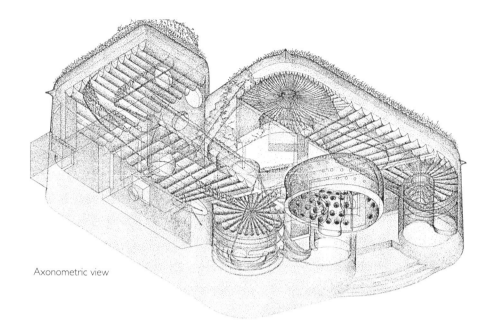

Axonometric view

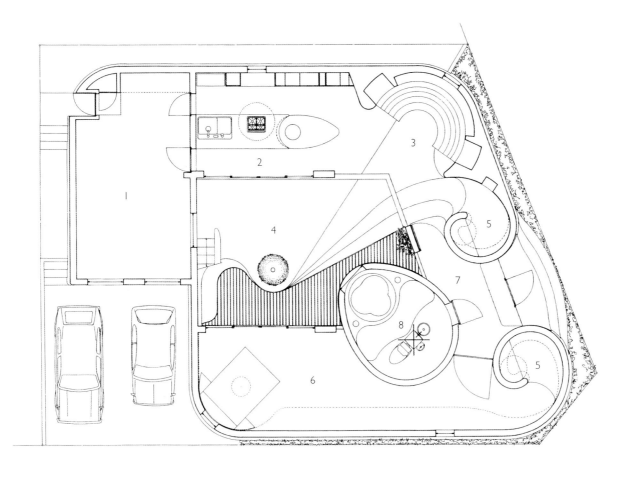

Floor plans

1. Play room
2. Dining-kitchen
3. Living
4. Courtyard
5. Study
6. Bedroom
7. Entrance
8. Bathroom

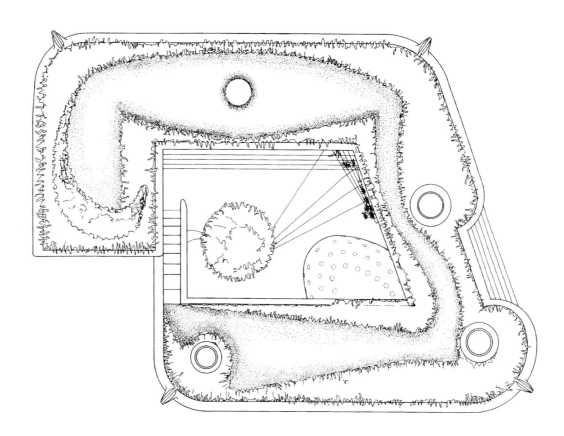

Elevations

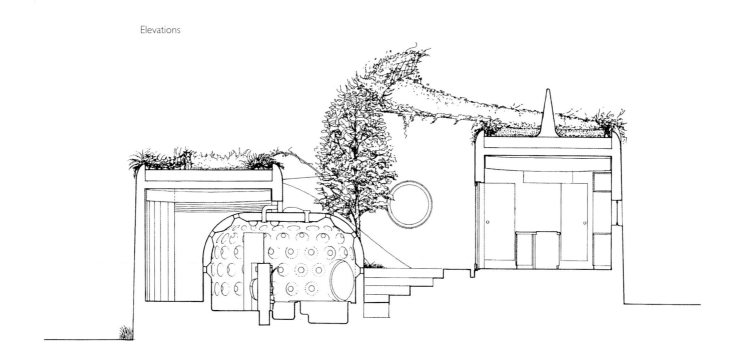

The bathroom has been designed in a curious spherical shape. Its placement, in a corner of the dwelling's inner patio, allows it to directly receive the natural light which filters through the small openings covering the surface.

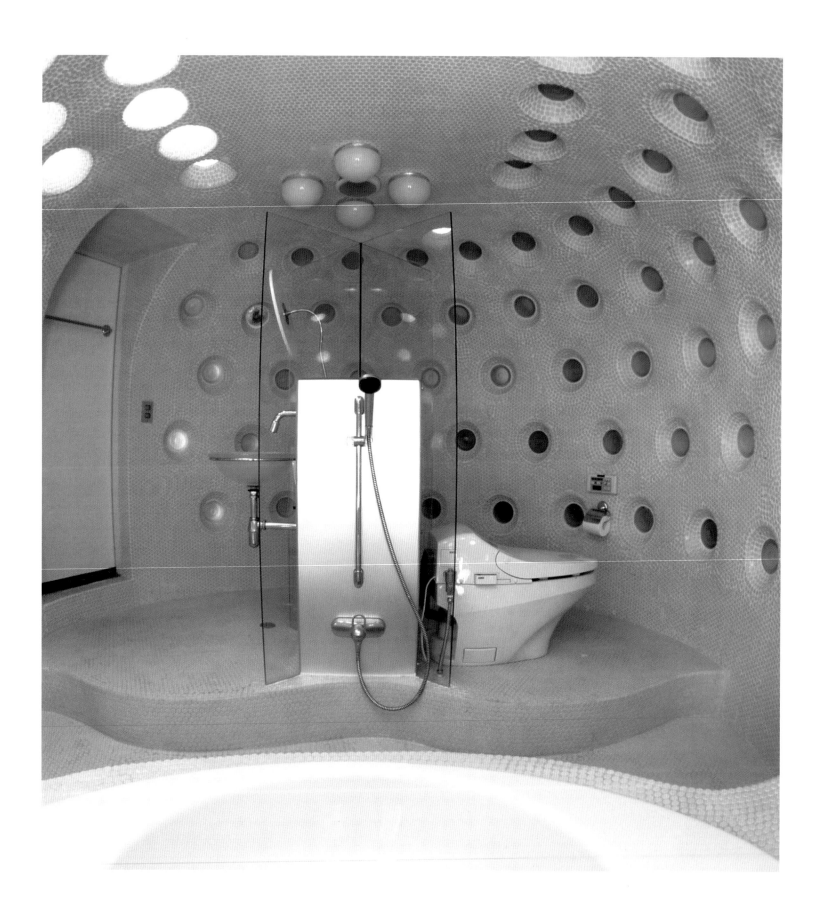